Passwords Diary

Copyright © 2014 YesWorkatHome.com
All rights reserved.
ISBN-13: 978-1479196661
ISBN-10: 1479196665

DEDICATION

To all of you that would like to know what to do with so many passwords to remember

ACKNOWLEDGMENTS

I will want to give thanks to the Giver of all of the ideas; the Lord Jesus Christ, who has place this book in my mind.
To my Son
My Mom
My Brothers and Sisters
And my Friends for their patience

CONTENTS

Organizing Your Passwords by Subject Title from A-Z

	Pg
	#6
A..	#13
B..	#20
C..	#27
D..	#34
E..	#41
F..	#48
G..	#55
H..	#62
I...	#69
J...	#76
K..	#83
L..	#90
M...	#97
N..	#104
O..	#111
P..	#118
Q...	#125
R..	#132
S..	#139
T..	#146
U..	#153
V..	#159
W...	#165
X..	#171
Y..	#177
Z..	
	#183
Business Info Organization.	#191
Website Info. Organization	#199
Self Notes	

Password Diary

 SUBJECT

Web Address	Phone
Email 2 Contact	
User Name	
Psw:	Fax
Q&A	
Comments	

Web Address	Phone
Email 2 Contact	
User Name	
Psw:	Fax
Q&A	
Comments	

Web Address	Phone
Email 2 Contact	
User Name	
Psw:	Fax
Q&A	
Comments	

Web Address	Phone
Email 2 Contact	
User Name	
Psw:	Fax
Q&A	
Comments	

Web Address	Phone
Email 2 Contact	
User Name	
Psw:	Fax
Q&A	
Comments	

Password Diary

SUBJECT A

Web Address	Phone

Email 2 Contact

User Name

Psw	Fax

Q&A

Comments

Web Address	Phone

Email 2 Contact

User Name

Psw	Fax

Q&A

Comments

Web Address	Phone

Email 2 Contact

User Name

Psw	Fax

Q&A

Comments

Web Address	Phone

Email 2 Contact

User Name

Psw	Fax

Q&A

Comments

Web Address	Phone

Email 2 Contact

User Name

Psw	Fax

Q&A

Comments

Password Diary

 SUBJECT

Web Address	Phone

Email 2 Contact

User Name

Psw:	Fax

Q&A

Comments

Web Address	Phone

Email 2 Contact

User Name

Psw:	Fax

Q&A

Comments

Web Address	Phone

Email 2 Contact

User Name

Psw:	Fax

Q&A

Comments

Web Address	Phone

Email 2 Contact

User Name

Psw:	Fax

Q&A

Comments

Web Address	Phone

Email 2 Contact

User Name

Psw:	Fax

Q&A

Comments

Password Diary

SUBJECT

A

Web Address	Phone

Email 2 Contact

User Name

Psw	Fax

Q&A

Comments

Web Address	Phone

Email 2 Contact

User Name

Psw	Fax

Q&A

Comments

Web Address	Phone

Email 2 Contact

User Name

Psw	Fax

Q&A

Comments

Web Address	Phone

Email 2 Contact

User Name

Psw	Fax

Q&A

Comments

Web Address	Phone

Email 2 Contact

User Name

Psw	Fax

Q&A

Comments

Password Diary

A SUBJECT

Web Address	Phone

Email 2 Contact

User Name

Psw:	Fax

Q&A

Comments

Web Address	Phone

Email 2 Contact

User Name

Psw:	Fax

Q&A

Comments

Web Address	Phone

Email 2 Contact

User Name

Psw:	Fax

Q&A

Comments

Web Address	Phone

Email 2 Contact

User Name

Psw:	Fax

Q&A

Comments

Web Address	Phone

Email 2 Contact

User Name

Psw:	Fax

Q&A

Comments

Password Diary

SUBJECT — A

Web Address	Phone
Email 2 Contact	
User Name	
Psw:	Fax
Q&A	
Comments	

Web Address	Phone
Email 2 Contact	
User Name	
Psw:	Fax
Q&A	
Comments	

Web Address	Phone
Email 2 Contact	
User Name	
Psw:	Fax
Q&A	
Comments	

Web Address	Phone
Email 2 Contact	
User Name	
Psw:	Fax
Q&A	
Comments	

Web Address	Phone
Email 2 Contact	
User Name	
Psw:	Fax
Q&A	
Comments	

Password Diary

A — SUBJECT

Web Address	Phone

Email 2 Contact

User Name

Psw:	Fax

Q&A

Comments

Web Address	Phone

Email 2 Contact

User Name

Psw:	Fax

Q&A

Comments

Web Address	Phone

Email 2 Contact

User Name

Psw:	Fax

Q&A

Comments

Web Address	Phone

Email 2 Contact

User Name

Psw:	Fax

Q&A

Comments

Web Address	Phone

Email 2 Contact

User Name

Psw:	Fax

Q&A

Comments

Password Diary

SUBJECT

B

Web Address	Phone
Email 2 Contact	
User Name	
Psw	Fax
Q&A	
Comments	
Web Address	Phone
Email 2 Contact	
User Name	
Psw	Fax
Q&A	
Comments	
Web Address	Phone
Email 2 Contact	
User Name	
Psw	Fax
Q&A	
Comments	
Web Address	Phone
Email 2 Contact	
User Name	
Psw	Fax
Q&A	
Comments	
Web Address	Phone
Email 2 Contact	
User Name	
Psw	Fax
Q&A	
Comments	

Password Diary

SUBJECT

B

Web Address	Phone
Email 2 Contact	
User Name	
Psw:	Fax
Q&A	
Comments	

Web Address	Phone
Email 2 Contact	
User Name	
Psw:	Fax
Q&A	
Comments	

Web Address	Phone
Email 2 Contact	
User Name	
Psw:	Fax
Q&A	
Comments	

Web Address	Phone
Email 2 Contact	
User Name	
Psw:	Fax
Q&A	
Comments	

Web Address	Phone
Email 2 Contact	
User Name	
Psw:	Fax
Q&A	
Comments	

Password Diary

SUBJECT

Web Address	Phone
Email 2 Contact	
User Name	
Psw:	Fax
Q&A	
Comments	
Web Address	Phone
Email 2 Contact	
User Name	
Psw:	Fax
Q&A	
Comments	
Web Address	Phone
Email 2 Contact	
User Name	
Psw:	Fax
Q&A	
Comments	
Web Address	Phone
Email 2 Contact	
User Name	
Psw:	Fax
Q&A	
Comments	
Web Address	Phone
Email 2 Contact	
User Name	
Psw:	Fax
Q&A	
Comments	

Password Diary

SUBJECT

B

Web Address	Phone
Email 2 Contact	
User Name	
Psw	Fax
Q&A	
Comments	

Web Address	Phone
Email 2 Contact	
User Name	
Psw	Fax
Q&A	
Comments	

Web Address	Phone
Email 2 Contact	
User Name	
Psw	Fax
Q&A	
Comments	

Web Address	Phone
Email 2 Contact	
User Name	
Psw	Fax
Q&A	
Comments	

Web Address	Phone
Email 2 Contact	
User Name	
Psw	Fax
Q&A	
Comments	

Password Diary

SUBJECT

B

Web Address	Phone
Email 2 Contact	
User Name	
Psw.	Fax
Q&A	
Comments	
Web Address	Phone
Email 2 Contact	
User Name	
Psw.	Fax
Q&A	
Comments	
Web Address	Phone
Email 2 Contact	
User Name	
Psw.	Fax
Q&A	
Comments	
Web Address	Phone
Email 2 Contact	
User Name	
Psw.	Fax
Q&A	
Comments	
Web Address	Phone
Email 2 Contact	
User Name	
Psw.	Fax
Q&A	
Comments	

Password Diary

SUBJECT

B

Web Address	Phone
Email 2 Contact	
User Name	
Psw:	Fax
Q&A	
Comments	

Web Address	Phone
Email 2 Contact	
User Name	
Psw	Fax
Q&A	
Comments	

Web Address	Phone
Email 2 Contact	
User Name	
Psw.	Fax
Q&A	
Comments	

Web Address	Phone
Email 2 Contact	
User Name	
Psw:	Fax
Q&A	
Comments	

Web Address	Phone
Email 2 Contact	
User Name	
Psw.	Fax
Q&A	
Comments	

Password Diary

SUBJECT

Web Address	Phone
Email 2 Contact	
User Name	
Psw	Fax
Q&A	
Comments	
Web Address	Phone
Email 2 Contact	
User Name	
Psw	Fax
Q&A	
Comments	
Web Address	Phone
Email 2 Contact	
User Name	
Psw	Fax
Q&A	
Comments	
Web Address	Phone
Email 2 Contact	
User Name	
Psw	Fax
Q&A	
Comments	
Web Address	Phone
Email 2 Contact	
User Name	
Psw	Fax
Q&A	
Comments	

B

Password Diary

C

SUBJECT

Web Address	Phone
Email 2 Contact	
User Name	
Psw:	Fax
Q&A	
Comments	

Web Address	Phone
Email 2 Contact	
User Name	
Psw:	Fax
Q&A	
Comments	

Web Address	Phone
Email 2 Contact	
User Name	
Psw:	Fax
Q&A	
Comments	

Web Address	Phone
Email 2 Contact	
User Name	
Psw:	Fax
Q&A	
Comments	

Web Address	Phone
Email 2 Contact	
User Name	
Psw:	Fax
Q&A	
Comments	

Password Diary

SUBJECT

C

Web Address	Phone
Email 2 Contact	
User Name	
Psw	Fax
Q&A	
Comments	

Web Address	Phone
Email 2 Contact	
User Name	
Psw	Fax
Q&A	
Comments	

Web Address	Phone
Email 2 Contact	
User Name	
Psw	Fax
Q&A	
Comments	

Web Address	Phone
Email 2 Contact	
User Name	
Psw	Fax
Q&A	
Comments	

Web Address	Phone
Email 2 Contact	
User Name	
Psw	Fax
Q&A	
Comments	

Password Diary

SUBJECT

C

Web Address	Phone
Email 2 Contact	
User Name	
Psw:	Fax
Q&A	
Comments	

Web Address	Phone
Email 2 Contact	
User Name	
Psw:	Fax
Q&A	
Comments	

Web Address	Phone
Email 2 Contact	
User Name	
Psw:	Fax
Q&A	
Comments	

Web Address	Phone
Email 2 Contact	
User Name	
Psw:	Fax
Q&A	
Comments	

Web Address	Phone
Email 2 Contact	
User Name	
Psw:	Fax
Q&A	
Comments	

Password Diary

SUBJECT

Web Address	Phone
Email 2 Contact	
User Name	
Psw:	Fax
Q&A	
Comments	

Web Address	Phone
Email 2 Contact	
User Name	
Psw:	Fax
Q&A	
Comments	

Web Address	Phone
Email 2 Contact	
User Name	
Psw:	Fax
Q&A	
Comments	

Web Address	Phone
Email 2 Contact	
User Name	
Psw:	Fax
Q&A	
Comments	

Web Address	Phone
Email 2 Contact	
User Name	
Psw:	Fax
Q&A	
Comments	

Password Diary

SUBJECT

C

Web Address	Phone
Email 2 Contact	
User Name	
Psw:	Fax
Q&A	
Comments	

Web Address	Phone
Email 2 Contact	
User Name	
Psw:	Fax
Q&A	
Comments	

Web Address	Phone
Email 2 Contact	
User Name	
Psw:	Fax
Q&A	
Comments	

Web Address	Phone
Email 2 Contact	
User Name	
Psw:	Fax
Q&A	
Comments	

Web Address	Phone
Email 2 Contact	
User Name	
Psw:	Fax
Q&A	
Comments	

Password Diary

SUBJECT

Web Address	Phone

Email 2 Contact

C

User Name

Psw	Fax

Q&A

Comments

Web Address	Phone

Email 2 Contact

User Name

Psw	Fax

Q&A

Comments

Web Address	Phone

Email 2 Contact

User Name

Psw	Fax

Q&A

Comments

Web Address	Phone

Email 2 Contact

User Name

Psw	Fax

Q&A

Comments

Web Address	Phone

Email 2 Contact

User Name

Psw	Fax

Q&A

Comments

Password Diary

SUBJECT

C

Web Address	Phone
Email 2 Contact	
User Name	
Psw:	Fax
Q&A	
Comments	

Web Address	Phone
Email 2 Contact	
User Name	
Psw:	Fax
Q&A	
Comments	

Web Address	Phone
Email 2 Contact	
User Name	
Psw:	Fax
Q&A	
Comments	

Web Address	Phone
Email 2 Contact	
User Name	
Psw:	Fax
Q&A	
Comments	

Web Address	Phone
Email 2 Contact	
User Name	
Psw:	Fax
Q&A	
Comments	

Password Diary

SUBJECT

Web Address	Phone
Email 2 Contact	
User Name	
Psw:	Fax
Q&A	
Comments	

D

Web Address	Phone
Email 2 Contact	
User Name	
Psw:	Fax
Q&A	
Comments	

Web Address	Phone
Email 2 Contact	
User Name	
Psw:	Fax
Q&A	
Comments	

Web Address	Phone
Email 2 Contact	
User Name	
Psw:	Fax
Q&A	
Comments	

Web Address	Phone
Email 2 Contact	
User Name	
Psw:	Fax
Q&A	
Comments	

Password Diary

SUBJECT

D

Web Address	Phone
Email 2 Contact	
User Name	
Psw	Fax
Q&A	
Comments	

Web Address	Phone
Email 2 Contact	
User Name	
Psw	Fax
Q&A	
Comments	

Web Address	Phone
Email 2 Contact	
User Name	
Psw	Fax
Q&A	
Comments	

Web Address	Phone
Email 2 Contact	
User Name	
Psw	Fax
Q&A	
Comments	

Web Address	Phone
Email 2 Contact	
User Name	
Psw	Fax
Q&A	
Comments	

Password Diary

SUBJECT

Web Address	Phone

Email 2 Contact

User Name

D

Psw	Fax

Q&A

Comments

Web Address	Phone

Email 2 Contact

User Name

Psw	Fax

Q&A

Comments

Web Address	Phone

Email 2 Contact

User Name

Psw	Fax

Q&A

Comments

Web Address	Phone

Email 2 Contact

User Name

Psw	Fax

Q&A

Comments

Web Address	Phone

Email 2 Contact

User Name

Psw	Fax

Q&A

Comments

Password Diary

SUBJECT

D

Web Address	Phone
Email 2 Contact	
User Name	
Psw:	Fax
Q&A	
Comments	

Web Address	Phone
Email 2 Contact	
User Name	
Psw:	Fax
Q&A	
Comments	

Web Address	Phone
Email 2 Contact	
User Name	
Psw:	Fax
Q&A	
Comments	

Web Address	Phone
Email 2 Contact	
User Name	
Psw:	Fax
Q&A	
Comments	

Web Address	Phone
Email 2 Contact	
User Name	
Psw:	Fax
Q&A	
Comments	

Password Diary

SUBJECT

Web Address	Phone

Email 2 Contact

User Name

D

Psw	Fax

Q&A

Comments

Web Address	Phone

Email 2 Contact

User Name

Psw	Fax

Q&A

Comments

Web Address	Phone

Email 2 Contact

User Name

Psw	Fax

Q&A

Comments

Web Address	Phone

Email 2 Contact

User Name

Psw	Fax

Q&A

Comments

Web Address	Phone

Email 2 Contact

User Name

Psw	Fax

Q&A

Comments

Password Diary

SUBJECT

D

Web Address	Phone
Email 2 Contact	
User Name	
Psw:	Fax
Q&A	
Comments	

Web Address	Phone
Email 2 Contact	
User Name	
Psw:	Fax
Q&A	
Comments	

Web Address	Phone
Email 2 Contact	
User Name	
Psw:	Fax
Q&A	
Comments	

Web Address	Phone
Email 2 Contact	
User Name	
Psw:	Fax
Q&A	
Comments	

Web Address	Phone
Email 2 Contact	
User Name	
Psw:	Fax
Q&A	
Comments	

Password Diary

SUBJECT

Web Address	Phone
Email 2 Contact	
User Name	
Psw	Fax
Q&A	
Comments	

Web Address	Phone
Email 2 Contact	
User Name	
Psw	Fax
Q&A	
Comments	

Web Address	Phone
Email 2 Contact	
User Name	
Psw	Fax
Q&A	
Comments	

Web Address	Phone
Email 2 Contact	
User Name	
Psw	Fax
Q&A	
Comments	

Web Address	Phone
Email 2 Contact	
User Name	
Psw	Fax
Q&A	
Comments	

D

Password Diary

SUBJECT

E

Web Address	Phone
Email 2 Contact	
User Name	
Psw:	Fax
Q&A	
Comments	

Web Address	Phone
Email 2 Contact	
User Name	
Psw:	Fax
Q&A	
Comments	

Web Address	Phone
Email 2 Contact	
User Name	
Psw:	Fax
Q&A	
Comments	

Web Address	Phone
Email 2 Contact	
User Name	
Psw:	Fax
Q&A	
Comments	

Web Address	Phone
Email 2 Contact	
User Name	
Psw:	Fax
Q&A	
Comments	

Password Diary

SUBJECT

Web Address	Phone
Email 2 Contact	
User Name	
Psw:	Fax
Q&A	
Comments	

Web Address	Phone
Email 2 Contact	
User Name	
Psw:	Fax
Q&A	
Comments	

Web Address	Phone
Email 2 Contact	
User Name	
Psw:	Fax
Q&A	
Comments	

Web Address	Phone
Email 2 Contact	
User Name	
Psw:	Fax
Q&A	
Comments	

Web Address	Phone
Email 2 Contact	
User Name	
Psw:	Fax
Q&A	
Comments	

E

Password Diary

SUBJECT

Web Address	Phone
Email 2 Contact	
User Name	
Psw:	Fax
Q&A	
Comments	

Web Address	Phone
Email 2 Contact	
User Name	
Psw:	Fax
Q&A	
Comments	

Web Address	Phone
Email 2 Contact	
User Name	
Psw:	Fax
Q&A	
Comments	

Web Address	Phone
Email 2 Contact	
User Name	
Psw:	Fax
Q&A	
Comments	

Web Address	Phone
Email 2 Contact	
User Name	
Psw:	Fax
Q&A	
Comments	

Password Diary

SUBJECT

Web Address	Phone

Email 2 Contact

User Name

Psw:	Fax

Q&A

Comments

Web Address	Phone

Email 2 Contact

User Name

Psw:	Fax

Q&A

Comments

Web Address	Phone

Email 2 Contact

User Name

Psw:	Fax

Q&A

Comments

Web Address	Phone

Email 2 Contact

User Name

Psw:	Fax

Q&A

Comments

Web Address	Phone

Email 2 Contact

User Name

Psw:	Fax

Q&A

Comments

Password Diary

SUBJECT

Web Address	Phone
Email 2 Contact	
User Name	
Psw:	Fax
Q&A	
Comments	

Web Address	Phone
Email 2 Contact	
User Name	
Psw:	Fax
Q&A	
Comments	

Web Address	Phone
Email 2 Contact	
User Name	
Psw:	Fax
Q&A	
Comments	

Web Address	Phone
Email 2 Contact	
User Name	
Psw:	Fax
Q&A	
Comments	

Web Address	Phone
Email 2 Contact	
User Name	
Psw:	Fax
Q&A	
Comments	

Password Diary

SUBJECT

Web Address	Phone

Email 2 Contact

User Name

Psw:	Fax

Q&A

Comments

Web Address	Phone

Email 2 Contact

User Name

Psw:	Fax

Q&A

Comments

Web Address	Phone

Email 2 Contact

User Name

Psw:	Fax

Q&A

Comments

Web Address	Phone

Email 2 Contact

User Name

Psw:	Fax

Q&A

Comments

Web Address	Phone

Email 2 Contact

User Name

Psw:	Fax

Q&A

Comments

Password Diary

SUBJECT

Web Address	Phone

Email 2 Contact

User Name

E
Psw:	Fax

Q&A

Comments

Web Address	Phone

Email 2 Contact

User Name

Psw:	Fax

Q&A

Comments

Web Address	Phone

Email 2 Contact

User Name

Psw:	Fax

Q&A

Comments

Web Address	Phone

Email 2 Contact

User Name

Psw:	Fax

Q&A

Comments

Web Address	Phone

Email 2 Contact

User Name

Psw:	Fax

Q&A

Comments

Password Diary

SUBJECT

Web Address	Phone
Email 2 Contact	
User Name	
Psw.	Fax
Q&A	
Comments	
Web Address	Phone
Email 2 Contact	
User Name	
Psw.	Fax
Q&A	
Comments	
Web Address	Phone
Email 2 Contact	
User Name	
Psw.	Fax
Q&A	
Comments	
Web Address	Phone
Email 2 Contact	
User Name	
Psw.	Fax
Q&A	
Comments	
Web Address	Phone
Email 2 Contact	
User Name	
Psw.	Fax
Q&A	
Comments	

F

Password Diary

SUBJECT

F

Web Address	Phone
Email 2 Contact	
User Name	
Psw:	Fax
Q&A	
Comments	

Web Address	Phone
Email 2 Contact	
User Name	
Psw:	Fax
Q&A	
Comments	

Web Address	Phone
Email 2 Contact	
User Name	
Psw:	Fax
Q&A	
Comments	

Web Address	Phone
Email 2 Contact	
User Name	
Psw:	Fax
Q&A	
Comments	

Web Address	Phone
Email 2 Contact	
User Name	
Psw:	Fax
Q&A	
Comments	

Password Diary

SUBJECT

Web Address	Phone

Email 2 Contact

User Name

Psw	Fax

Q&A   **F**

Comments

Web Address	Phone

Email 2 Contact

User Name

Psw	Fax

Q&A

Comments

Web Address	Phone

Email 2 Contact

User Name

Psw	Fax

Q&A

Comments

Web Address	Phone

Email 2 Contact

User Name

Psw	Fax

Q&A

Comments

Web Address	Phone

Email 2 Contact

User Name

Psw	Fax

Q&A

Comments

Password Diary

SUBJECT

F

Web Address	Phone
Email 2 Contact	
User Name	
Psw:	Fax
Q&A	
Comments	

Web Address	Phone
Email 2 Contact	
User Name	
Psw:	Fax
Q&A	
Comments	

Web Address	Phone
Email 2 Contact	
User Name	
Psw:	Fax
Q&A	
Comments	

Web Address	Phone
Email 2 Contact	
User Name	
Psw:	Fax
Q&A	
Comments	

Web Address	Phone
Email 2 Contact	
User Name	
Psw:	Fax
Q&A	
Comments	

Password Diary

SUBJECT

| Web Address | Phone |
|---|---|//
Email 2 Contact	
User Name	
Psw.	Fax
Q&A	
Comments	

Web Address	Phone
Email 2 Contact	
User Name	
Psw.	Fax
Q&A	
Comments	

Web Address	Phone
Email 2 Contact	
User Name	
Psw.	Fax
Q&A	
Comments	

Web Address	Phone
Email 2 Contact	
User Name	
Psw.	Fax
Q&A	
Comments	

Web Address	Phone
Email 2 Contact	
User Name	
Psw.	Fax
Q&A	
Comments	

F

Password Diary

SUBJECT

Web Address	Phone
Email 2 Contact	
User Name	
Psw	Fax
Q&A	
Comments	

F

Web Address	Phone
Email 2 Contact	
User Name	
Psw	Fax
Q&A	
Comments	

Web Address	Phone
Email 2 Contact	
User Name	
Psw	Fax
Q&A	
Comments	

Web Address	Phone
Email 2 Contact	
User Name	
Psw	Fax
Q&A	
Comments	

Web Address	Phone
Email 2 Contact	
User Name	
Psw	Fax
Q&A	
Comments	

Password Diary

SUBJECT

Web Address	Phone
Email 2 Contact	
User Name	
Psw	Fax
Q&A	
Comments	

F

Web Address	Phone
Email 2 Contact	
User Name	
Psw	Fax
Q&A	
Comments	

Web Address	Phone
Email 2 Contact	
User Name	
Psw	Fax
Q&A	
Comments	

Web Address	Phone
Email 2 Contact	
User Name	
Psw	Fax
Q&A	
Comments	

Web Address	Phone
Email 2 Contact	
User Name	
Psw	Fax
Q&A	
Comments	

Password Diary

SUBJECT

Web Address	Phone
Email 2 Contact	
User Name	
Psw:	Fax
Q&A	

G Comments

Web Address	Phone
Email 2 Contact	
User Name	
Psw:	Fax
Q&A	

Comments

Web Address	Phone
Email 2 Contact	
User Name	
Psw:	Fax
Q&A	

Comments

Web Address	Phone
Email 2 Contact	
User Name	
Psw:	Fax
Q&A	

Comments

Web Address	Phone
Email 2 Contact	
User Name	
Psw:	Fax
Q&A	

Comments

Password Diary

SUBJECT

Web Address	Phone
Email 2 Contact	
User Name	
Psw	Fax
Q&A	
Comments	

G

Web Address	Phone
Email 2 Contact	
User Name	
Psw	Fax
Q&A	
Comments	

Web Address	Phone
Email 2 Contact	
User Name	
Psw	Fax
Q&A	
Comments	

Web Address	Phone
Email 2 Contact	
User Name	
Psw	Fax
Q&A	
Comments	

Web Address	Phone
Email 2 Contact	
User Name	
Psw	Fax
Q&A	
Comments	

Password Diary

SUBJECT

Web Address	Phone
Email 2 Contact	
User Name	
Psw:	Fax
Q&A	

G Comments

Web Address	Phone
Email 2 Contact	
User Name	
Psw:	Fax
Q&A	
Comments	

Web Address	Phone
Email 2 Contact	
User Name	
Psw:	Fax
Q&A	
Comments	

Web Address	Phone
Email 2 Contact	
User Name	
Psw:	Fax
Q&A	
Comments	

Web Address	Phone
Email 2 Contact	
User Name	
Psw:	Fax
Q&A	
Comments	

Password Diary

SUBJECT

Web Address	Phone

Email 2 Contact

User Name

Psw:	Fax

Q&A

Comments

G

Web Address	Phone

Email 2 Contact

User Name

Psw:	Fax

Q&A

Comments

Web Address	Phone

Email 2 Contact

User Name

Psw:	Fax

Q&A

Comments

Web Address	Phone

Email 2 Contact

User Name

Psw:	Fax

Q&A

Comments

Web Address	Phone

Email 2 Contact

User Name

Psw:	Fax

Q&A

Comments

Password Diary

SUBJECT

Web Address	Phone
Email 2 Contact	
User Name	
Psw:	Fax
Q&A	

G Comments

Web Address	Phone
Email 2 Contact	
User Name	
Psw	Fax
Q&A	

Comments

Web Address	Phone
Email 2 Contact	
User Name	
Psw:	Fax
Q&A	

Comments

Web Address	Phone
Email 2 Contact	
User Name	
Psw:	Fax
Q&A	

Comments

Web Address	Phone
Email 2 Contact	
User Name	
Psw:	Fax
Q&A	

Comments

Password Diary

SUBJECT

Web Address	Phone
Email 2 Contact	
User Name	
Psw.	Fax
Q&A	
Comments	

G

Web Address	Phone
Email 2 Contact	
User Name	
Psw.	Fax
Q&A	
Comments	

Web Address	Phone
Email 2 Contact	
User Name	
Psw.	Fax
Q&A	
Comments	

Web Address	Phone
Email 2 Contact	
User Name	
Psw.	Fax
Q&A	
Comments	

Web Address	Phone
Email 2 Contact	
User Name	
Psw.	Fax
Q&A	
Comments	

Password Diary

SUBJECT

Web Address	Phone
Email 2 Contact	
User Name	
Psw:	Fax
Q&A	

G Comments

Web Address	Phone
Email 2 Contact	
User Name	
Psw:	Fax
Q&A	

Comments

Web Address	Phone
Email 2 Contact	
User Name	
Psw:	Fax
Q&A	

Comments

Web Address	Phone
Email 2 Contact	
User Name	
Psw:	Fax
Q&A	

Comments

Web Address	Phone
Email 2 Contact	
User Name	
Psw:	Fax
Q&A	

Comments

Password Diary

SUBJECT

Web Address	Phone
Email 2 Contact	
User Name	
Psw	Fax
Q&A	
Comments	

Web Address	Phone
Email 2 Contact	
User Name	
Psw	Fax
Q&A	
Comments	

Web Address	Phone
Email 2 Contact	
User Name	
Psw	Fax
Q&A	
Comments	

Web Address	Phone
Email 2 Contact	
User Name	
Psw	Fax
Q&A	
Comments	

Web Address	Phone
Email 2 Contact	
User Name	
Psw	Fax
Q&A	
Comments	

H

Password Diary

SUBJECT

Web Address	Phone
Email 2 Contact	
User Name	
Psw:	Fax
Q&A	
Comments	

H

Web Address	Phone
Email 2 Contact	
User Name	
Psw:	Fax
Q&A	
Comments	

Web Address	Phone
Email 2 Contact	
User Name	
Psw:	Fax
Q&A	
Comments	

Web Address	Phone
Email 2 Contact	
User Name	
Psw:	Fax
Q&A	
Comments	

Web Address	Phone
Email 2 Contact	
User Name	
Psw:	Fax
Q&A	
Comments	

Password Diary

SUBJECT

Web Address	Phone

Email 2 Contact

User Name

Psw.	Fax

Q&A

Comments

Web Address	Phone

Email 2 Contact

User Name

Psw.	Fax

Q&A

Comments

Web Address	Phone

Email 2 Contact

User Name

Psw.	Fax

Q&A

Comments

Web Address	Phone

Email 2 Contact

User Name

Psw.	Fax

Q&A

Comments

Web Address	Phone

Email 2 Contact

User Name

Psw.	Fax

Q&A

Comments

H

Password Diary

SUBJECT

Web Address	Phone
Email 2 Contact	
User Name	
Psw:	Fax
Q&A	
Comments	

H

Web Address	Phone
Email 2 Contact	
User Name	
Psw:	Fax
Q&A	
Comments	

Web Address	Phone
Email 2 Contact	
User Name	
Psw:	Fax
Q&A	
Comments	

Web Address	Phone
Email 2 Contact	
User Name	
Psw:	Fax
Q&A	
Comments	

Web Address	Phone
Email 2 Contact	
User Name	
Psw:	Fax
Q&A	
Comments	

Password Diary

SUBJECT

Web Address	Phone
Email 2 Contact	
User Name	
Psw:	Fax
Q&A	
Comments	

Web Address	Phone
Email 2 Contact	
User Name	
Psw:	Fax
Q&A	
Comments	

Web Address	Phone
Email 2 Contact	
User Name	
Psw:	Fax
Q&A	
Comments	

Web Address	Phone
Email 2 Contact	
User Name	
Psw:	Fax
Q&A	
Comments	

Web Address	Phone
Email 2 Contact	
User Name	
Psw:	Fax
Q&A	
Comments	

H

Password Diary

SUBJECT

Web Address	Phone
Email 2 Contact	
User Name	
Psw:	Fax
Q&A	
Comments	

H

Web Address	Phone
Email 2 Contact	
User Name	
Psw:	Fax
Q&A	
Comments	

Web Address	Phone
Email 2 Contact	
User Name	
Psw:	Fax
Q&A	
Comments	

Web Address	Phone
Email 2 Contact	
User Name	
Psw:	Fax
Q&A	
Comments	

Web Address	Phone
Email 2 Contact	
User Name	
Psw:	Fax
Q&A	
Comments	

Password Diary

SUBJECT

Web Address	Phone
Email 2 Contact	
User Name	
Psw:	Fax
Q&A	
Comments	

Web Address	Phone
Email 2 Contact	
User Name	
Psw:	Fax
Q&A	
Comments	

Web Address	Phone
Email 2 Contact	
User Name	
Psw:	Fax
Q&A	
Comments	

Web Address	Phone
Email 2 Contact	
User Name	
Psw:	Fax
Q&A	
Comments	

Web Address	Phone
Email 2 Contact	
User Name	
Psw:	Fax
Q&A	
Comments	

H

Password Diary

SUBJECT

Web Address	Phone
Email 2 Contact	
User Name	
Psw:	Fax
Q&A	
Comments	
Web Address	Phone
Email 2 Contact	
User Name	
Psw:	Fax
Q&A	
Comments	
Web Address	Phone
Email 2 Contact	
User Name	
Psw:	Fax
Q&A	
Comments	
Web Address	Phone
Email 2 Contact	
User Name	
Psw:	Fax
Q&A	
Comments	
Web Address	Phone
Email 2 Contact	
User Name	
Psw:	Fax
Q&A	
Comments	

I

Password Diary

SUBJECT

Web Address	Phone
Email 2 Contact	
User Name	
Psw	Fax
Q&A	
Comments	

Web Address	Phone
Email 2 Contact	
User Name	
Psw	Fax
Q&A	
Comments	

Web Address	Phone
Email 2 Contact	
User Name	
Psw	Fax
Q&A	
Comments	

Web Address	Phone
Email 2 Contact	
User Name	
Psw	Fax
Q&A	
Comments	

Web Address	Phone
Email 2 Contact	
User Name	
Psw	Fax
Q&A	
Comments	

Password Diary

SUBJECT

Web Address	Phone
Email 2 Contact	
User Name	
Psw:	Fax
Q&A	
Comments	

Web Address	Phone
Email 2 Contact	
User Name	
Psw:	Fax
Q&A	
Comments	

Web Address	Phone
Email 2 Contact	
User Name	
Psw:	Fax
Q&A	
Comments	

Web Address	Phone
Email 2 Contact	
User Name	
Psw:	Fax
Q&A	
Comments	

Web Address	Phone
Email 2 Contact	
User Name	
Psw:	Fax
Q&A	
Comments	

Password Diary

SUBJECT

Web Address	Phone

Email 2 Contact

User Name

Psw	Fax

Q&A

Comments

Web Address	Phone

Email 2 Contact

User Name

Psw	Fax

Q&A

Comments

Web Address	Phone

Email 2 Contact

User Name

Psw	Fax

Q&A

Comments

Web Address	Phone

Email 2 Contact

User Name

Psw	Fax

Q&A

Comments

Web Address	Phone

Email 2 Contact

User Name

Psw	Fax

Q&A

Comments

Password Diary

SUBJECT

Web Address	Phone
Email 2 Contact	
User Name	
Psw:	Fax
Q&A	
Comments	

Web Address	Phone
Email 2 Contact	
User Name	
Psw:	Fax
Q&A	
Comments	

Web Address	Phone
Email 2 Contact	
User Name	
Psw:	Fax
Q&A	
Comments	

Web Address	Phone
Email 2 Contact	
User Name	
Psw:	Fax
Q&A	
Comments	

Web Address	Phone
Email 2 Contact	
User Name	
Psw:	Fax
Q&A	
Comments	

Password Diary

SUBJECT

Web Address	Phone
Email 2 Contact	
User Name	
Psw	Fax
Q&A	
Comments	
Web Address	Phone
Email 2 Contact	
User Name	
Psw	Fax
Q&A	
Comments	
Web Address	Phone
Email 2 Contact	
User Name	
Psw	Fax
Q&A	
Comments	
Web Address	Phone
Email 2 Contact	
User Name	
Psw	Fax
Q&A	
Comments	
Web Address	Phone
Email 2 Contact	
User Name	
Psw	Fax
Q&A	
Comments	

I

Password Diary

SUBJECT

Web Address	Phone
Email 2 Contact	
User Name	
Psw:	Fax
Q&A	
Comments	

Web Address	Phone
Email 2 Contact	
User Name	
Psw:	Fax
Q&A	
Comments	

Web Address	Phone
Email 2 Contact	
User Name	
Psw:	Fax
Q&A	
Comments	

Web Address	Phone
Email 2 Contact	
User Name	
Psw:	Fax
Q&A	
Comments	

Web Address	Phone
Email 2 Contact	
User Name	
Psw:	Fax
Q&A	
Comments	

I

Password Diary

SUBJECT

Web Address	Phone
Email 2 Contact	
User Name	
Psw:	Fax
Q&A	
Comments	

Web Address	Phone
Email 2 Contact	
User Name	
Psw:	Fax
Q&A	
Comments	

Web Address	Phone
Email 2 Contact	
User Name	
Psw:	Fax
Q&A	
Comments	

Web Address	Phone
Email 2 Contact	
User Name	
Psw:	Fax
Q&A	
Comments	

Web Address	Phone
Email 2 Contact	
User Name	
Psw:	Fax
Q&A	
Comments	

J

Password Diary

SUBJECT

Web Address	Phone

Email 2 Contact

User Name

Psw:	Fax

Q&A

Comments

Web Address	Phone

Email 2 Contact

J User Name

Psw:	Fax

Q&A

Comments

Web Address	Phone

Email 2 Contact

User Name

Psw:	Fax

Q&A

Comments

Web Address	Phone

Email 2 Contact

User Name

Psw:	Fax

Q&A

Comments

Web Address	Phone

Email 2 Contact

User Name

Psw:	Fax

Q&A

Comments

Password Diary

SUBJECT

Web Address	Phone

Email 2 Contact

User Name

Psw:	Fax

Q&A

Comments

Web Address	Phone

Email 2 Contact

User Name

J

Psw:	Fax

Q&A

Comments

Web Address	Phone

Email 2 Contact

User Name

Psw:	Fax

Q&A

Comments

Web Address	Phone

Email 2 Contact

User Name

Psw:	Fax

Q&A

Comments

Web Address	Phone

Email 2 Contact

User Name

Psw:	Fax

Q&A

Comments

Password Diary

SUBJECT

Web Address	Phone
Email 2 Contact	
User Name	
Psw:	Fax
Q&A	
Comments	

Web Address	Phone
Email 2 Contact	
User Name	
Psw:	Fax
Q&A	
Comments	

J

Web Address	Phone
Email 2 Contact	
User Name	
Psw:	Fax
Q&A	
Comments	

Web Address	Phone
Email 2 Contact	
User Name	
Psw:	Fax
Q&A	
Comments	

Web Address	Phone
Email 2 Contact	
User Name	
Psw:	Fax
Q&A	
Comments	

Password Diary

SUBJECT

Web Address	Phone

Email 2 Contact

User Name

Psw:	Fax

Q&A

Comments

Web Address	Phone

Email 2 Contact

User Name

J

Psw:	Fax

Q&A

Comments

Web Address	Phone

Email 2 Contact

User Name

Psw:	Fax

Q&A

Comments

Web Address	Phone

Email 2 Contact

User Name

Psw:	Fax

Q&A

Comments

Web Address	Phone

Email 2 Contact

User Name

Psw:	Fax

Q&A

Comments

Password Diary

SUBJECT

Web Address	Phone
Email 2 Contact	
User Name	
Psw:	Fax
Q&A	
Comments	

Web Address	Phone
Email 2 Contact	
User Name	
Psw:	Fax
Q&A	
Comments	

J

Web Address	Phone
Email 2 Contact	
User Name	
Psw:	Fax
Q&A	
Comments	

Web Address	Phone
Email 2 Contact	
User Name	
Psw:	Fax
Q&A	
Comments	

Web Address	Phone
Email 2 Contact	
User Name	
Psw:	Fax
Q&A	
Comments	

Password Diary

SUBJECT

Web Address	Phone

Email 2 Contact

User Name

Psw	Fax

Q&A

Comments

Web Address	Phone

Email 2 Contact

User Name

Psw	Fax

Q&A

Comments

Web Address	Phone

Email 2 Contact

User Name

Psw	Fax

Q&A

Comments

Web Address	Phone

Email 2 Contact

User Name

Psw.	Fax

Q&A

Comments

Web Address	Phone

Email 2 Contact

User Name

Psw	Fax

Q&A

Comments

Password Diary

SUBJECT

Web Address	Phone
Email 2 Contact	
User Name	
Psw:	Fax
Q&A	
Comments	

Web Address	Phone
Email 2 Contact	
User Name	
Psw:	Fax
Q&A	
Comments	

K

Web Address	Phone
Email 2 Contact	
User Name	
Psw:	Fax
Q&A	
Comments	

Web Address	Phone
Email 2 Contact	
User Name	
Psw:	Fax
Q&A	
Comments	

Web Address	Phone
Email 2 Contact	
User Name	
Psw:	Fax
Q&A	
Comments	

Password Diary

SUBJECT

Web Address	Phone

Email 2 Contact

User Name

Psw:	Fax

Q&A

Comments

Web Address	Phone

Email 2 Contact

User Name

Psw:	Fax

Q&A

Comments

Web Address	Phone

Email 2 Contact

User Name

Psw:	Fax

Q&A

Comments

Web Address	Phone

Email 2 Contact

User Name

Psw:	Fax

Q&A

Comments

Web Address	Phone

Email 2 Contact

User Name

Psw:	Fax

Q&A

Comments

K

Password Diary

SUBJECT

Web Address	Phone
Email 2 Contact	
User Name	
Psw:	Fax
Q&A	
Comments	

Web Address	Phone
Email 2 Contact	
User Name	
Psw:	Fax
Q&A	
Comments	

K

Web Address	Phone
Email 2 Contact	
User Name	
Psw:	Fax
Q&A	
Comments	

Web Address	Phone
Email 2 Contact	
User Name	
Psw:	Fax
Q&A	
Comments	

Web Address	Phone
Email 2 Contact	
User Name	
Psw:	Fax
Q&A	
Comments	

Password Diary

SUBJECT

Web Address	Phone
Email 2 Contact	
User Name	
Psw	Fax
Q&A	
Comments	
Web Address	Phone
Email 2 Contact	
User Name	
Psw	Fax
Q&A	
Comments	
Web Address	Phone
Email 2 Contact	
User Name	
Psw	Fax
Q&A	
Comments	
Web Address	Phone
Email 2 Contact	
User Name	
Psw	Fax
Q&A	
Comments	
Web Address	Phone
Email 2 Contact	
User Name	
Psw	Fax
Q&A	
Comments	

K

Password Diary

SUBJECT

Web Address	Phone
Email 2 Contact	
User Name	
Psw:	Fax
Q&A	
Comments	

Web Address	Phone
Email 2 Contact	
User Name	
Psw:	Fax
Q&A	
Comments	

K

Web Address	Phone
Email 2 Contact	
User Name	
Psw:	Fax
Q&A	
Comments	

Web Address	Phone
Email 2 Contact	
User Name	
Psw:	Fax
Q&A	
Comments	

Web Address	Phone
Email 2 Contact	
User Name	
Psw:	Fax
Q&A	
Comments	

Password Diary

SUBJECT

Web Address	Phone

Email 2 Contact

User Name

Psw	Fax

Q&A

Comments

Web Address	Phone

Email 2 Contact

User Name

Psw	Fax

Q&A

Comments

K

Web Address	Phone

Email 2 Contact

User Name

Psw	Fax

Q&A

Comments

Web Address	Phone

Email 2 Contact

User Name

Psw	Fax

Q&A

Comments

Web Address	Phone

Email 2 Contact

User Name

Psw	Fax

Q&A

Comments

Password Diary

SUBJECT

Web Address	Phone
Email 2 Contact	
User Name	
Psw:	Fax
Q&A	
Comments	

Web Address	Phone
Email 2 Contact	
User Name	
Psw:	Fax
Q&A	
Comments	

K

Web Address	Phone
Email 2 Contact	
User Name	
Psw:	Fax
Q&A	
Comments	

Web Address	Phone
Email 2 Contact	
User Name	
Psw:	Fax
Q&A	
Comments	

Web Address	Phone
Email 2 Contact	
User Name	
Psw:	Fax
Q&A	
Comments	

Password Diary

SUBJECT

Web Address	Phone

Email 2 Contact

User Name

Psw:	Fax

Q&A

Comments

Web Address	Phone

Email 2 Contact

User Name

Psw:	Fax

Q&A

Comments

Web Address	Phone

Email 2 Contact

User Name

Psw:	Fax

Q&A

Comments

Web Address	Phone

Email 2 Contact

User Name

Psw:	Fax

Q&A

Comments

Web Address	Phone

Email 2 Contact

User Name

Psw:	Fax

Q&A

Comments

L

Password Diary

SUBJECT

Web Address	Phone
Email 2 Contact	
User Name	
Psw:	Fax
Q&A	
Comments	
Web Address	Phone
Email 2 Contact	
User Name	
Psw:	Fax
Q&A	
Comments	
Web Address	Phone
Email 2 Contact	
User Name	
Psw:	Fax
Q&A	
Comments	
Web Address	Phone
Email 2 Contact	
User Name	
Psw:	Fax
Q&A	
Comments	
Web Address	Phone
Email 2 Contact	
User Name	
Psw:	Fax
Q&A	
Comments	

L

Password Diary

SUBJECT

Web Address	Phone

Email 2 Contact

User Name

Psw	Fax

Q&A

Comments

Web Address	Phone

Email 2 Contact

User Name

Psw	Fax

Q&A

Comments

Web Address	Phone

Email 2 Contact

User Name

Psw	Fax

Q&A

Comments

Web Address	Phone

Email 2 Contact

User Name

Psw	Fax

Q&A

Comments

Web Address	Phone

Email 2 Contact

User Name

Psw	Fax

Q&A

Comments

L

Password Diary

SUBJECT

Web Address	Phone
Email 2 Contact	
User Name	
Psw:	Fax
Q&A	
Comments	

Web Address	Phone
Email 2 Contact	
User Name	
Psw:	Fax
Q&A	
Comments	

Web Address	Phone
Email 2 Contact	
User Name	
Psw:	Fax
Q&A	
Comments	

Web Address	Phone
Email 2 Contact	
User Name	
Psw:	Fax
Q&A	
Comments	

Web Address	Phone
Email 2 Contact	
User Name	
Psw:	Fax
Q&A	
Comments	

L

Password Diary

SUBJECT

Web Address	Phone
Email 2 Contact	
User Name	
Psw:	Fax
Q&A	
Comments	

Web Address	Phone
Email 2 Contact	
User Name	
Psw:	Fax
Q&A	
Comments	

Web Address	Phone
Email 2 Contact	
User Name	
Psw:	Fax
Q&A	
Comments	

Web Address	Phone
Email 2 Contact	
User Name	
Psw:	Fax
Q&A	
Comments	

Web Address	Phone
Email 2 Contact	
User Name	
Psw:	Fax
Q&A	
Comments	

L

Password Diary

SUBJECT

| Web Address | Phone |
|---|---|//
Email 2 Contact	
User Name	
Psw:	Fax
Q&A	
Comments	
Web Address	Phone
Email 2 Contact	
User Name	
Psw:	Fax
Q&A	
Comments	
Web Address	Phone
Email 2 Contact	
User Name	
Psw:	Fax
Q&A	
Comments	
Web Address	Phone
Email 2 Contact	
User Name	
Psw:	Fax
Q&A	
Comments	
Web Address	Phone
Email 2 Contact	
User Name	
Psw:	Fax
Q&A	
Comments	

L

Password Diary

SUBJECT

Web Address	Phone
Email 2 Contact	
User Name	
Psw:	Fax
Q&A	
Comments	
Web Address	Phone
Email 2 Contact	
User Name	
Psw:	Fax
Q&A	
Comments	
Web Address	Phone
Email 2 Contact	
User Name	
Psw:	Fax
Q&A	
Comments	
Web Address	Phone
Email 2 Contact	
User Name	
Psw:	Fax
Q&A	
Comments	
Web Address	Phone
Email 2 Contact	
User Name	
Psw:	Fax
Q&A	
Comments	

L

Password Diary

SUBJECT

Web Address	Phone
Email 2 Contact	
User Name	
Psw:	Fax
Q&A	
Comments	

Web Address	Phone
Email 2 Contact	
User Name	
Psw:	Fax
Q&A	
Comments	

M

Web Address	Phone
Email 2 Contact	
User Name	
Psw:	Fax
Q&A	
Comments	

Web Address	Phone
Email 2 Contact	
User Name	
Psw:	Fax
Q&A	
Comments	

Web Address	Phone
Email 2 Contact	
User Name	
Psw:	Fax
Q&A	
Comments	

Password Diary

SUBJECT

Web Address	Phone
Email 2 Contact	
User Name	
Psw	Fax
Q&A	
Comments	

Web Address	Phone
Email 2 Contact	
User Name	
Psw	Fax
Q&A	
Comments	

M

Web Address	Phone
Email 2 Contact	
User Name	
Psw	Fax
Q&A	
Comments	

Web Address	Phone
Email 2 Contact	
User Name	
Psw	Fax
Q&A	
Comments	

Web Address	Phone
Email 2 Contact	
User Name	
Psw	Fax
Q&A	
Comments	

Password Diary

SUBJECT

Web Address	Phone
Email 2 Contact	
User Name	
Psw:	Fax
Q&A	
Comments	

Web Address	Phone
Email 2 Contact	
User Name	
Psw:	Fax
Q&A	
Comments	

M

Web Address	Phone
Email 2 Contact	
User Name	
Psw:	Fax
Q&A	
Comments	

Web Address	Phone
Email 2 Contact	
User Name	
Psw:	Fax
Q&A	
Comments	

Web Address	Phone
Email 2 Contact	
User Name	
Psw:	Fax
Q&A	
Comments	

Password Diary

SUBJECT

Web Address	Phone

Email 2 Contact

User Name

Psw:	Fax

Q&A

Comments

Web Address	Phone

Email 2 Contact

User Name

Psw:	Fax

Q&A

Comments

M

Web Address	Phone

Email 2 Contact

User Name

Psw:	Fax

Q&A

Comments

Web Address	Phone

Email 2 Contact

User Name

Psw:	Fax

Q&A

Comments

Web Address	Phone

Email 2 Contact

User Name

Psw:	Fax

Q&A

Comments

Password Diary

SUBJECT

Web Address	Phone
Email 2 Contact	
User Name	
Psw:	Fax
Q&A	
Comments	

Web Address	Phone
Email 2 Contact	
User Name	
Psw:	Fax
Q&A	
Comments	

M

Web Address	Phone
Email 2 Contact	
User Name	
Psw:	Fax
Q&A	
Comments	

Web Address	Phone
Email 2 Contact	
User Name	
Psw:	Fax
Q&A	
Comments	

Web Address	Phone
Email 2 Contact	
User Name	
Psw:	Fax
Q&A	
Comments	

Password Diary

SUBJECT

Web Address	Phone

Email 2 Contact

User Name

Psw.	Fax

Q&A

Comments

Web Address	Phone

Email 2 Contact

User Name

Psw.	Fax

Q&A

Comments

M

Web Address	Phone

Email 2 Contact

User Name

Psw.	Fax

Q&A

Comments

Web Address	Phone

Email 2 Contact

User Name

Psw.	Fax

Q&A

Comments

Web Address	Phone

Email 2 Contact

User Name

Psw.	Fax

Q&A

Comments

Password Diary

SUBJECT

Web Address	Phone
Email 2 Contact	
User Name	
Psw:	Fax
Q&A	
Comments	

Web Address	Phone
Email 2 Contact	
User Name	
Psw:	Fax
Q&A	
Comments	

M

Web Address	Phone
Email 2 Contact	
User Name	
Psw:	Fax
Q&A	
Comments	

Web Address	Phone
Email 2 Contact	
User Name	
Psw:	Fax
Q&A	
Comments	

Web Address	Phone
Email 2 Contact	
User Name	
Psw:	Fax
Q&A	
Comments	

Password Diary

SUBJECT

Web Address	Phone

Email 2 Contact

User Name

Psw	Fax

Q&A

Comments

Web Address	Phone

Email 2 Contact

User Name

Psw	Fax

Q&A

Comments

Web Address	Phone

Email 2 Contact

User Name

Psw	Fax

Q&A

Comments

Web Address	Phone

Email 2 Contact

User Name

Psw	Fax

Q&A

Comments

Web Address	Phone

Email 2 Contact

User Name

Psw	Fax

Q&A

Comments

N

Password Diary

SUBJECT

Web Address	Phone
Email 2 Contact	
User Name	
Psw:	Fax
Q&A	
Comments	

Web Address	Phone
Email 2 Contact	
User Name	
Psw:	Fax
Q&A	
Comments	

N

Web Address	Phone
Email 2 Contact	
User Name	
Psw:	Fax
Q&A	
Comments	

Web Address	Phone
Email 2 Contact	
User Name	
Psw:	Fax
Q&A	
Comments	

Web Address	Phone
Email 2 Contact	
User Name	
Psw:	Fax
Q&A	
Comments	

Password Diary

SUBJECT

Web Address	Phone
Email 2 Contact	
User Name	
Psw:	Fax
Q&A	
Comments	
Web Address	Phone
Email 2 Contact	
User Name	
Psw:	Fax
Q&A	
Comments	
Web Address	Phone
Email 2 Contact	
User Name	
Psw:	Fax
Q&A	
Comments	
Web Address	Phone
Email 2 Contact	
User Name	
Psw:	Fax
Q&A	
Comments	
Web Address	Phone
Email 2 Contact	
User Name	
Psw:	Fax
Q&A	
Comments	

N

Password Diary

SUBJECT

Web Address	Phone
Email 2 Contact	
User Name	
Psw:	Fax
Q&A	
Comments	

Web Address	Phone
Email 2 Contact	
User Name	
Psw:	Fax
Q&A	
Comments	

N

Web Address	Phone
Email 2 Contact	
User Name	
Psw:	Fax
Q&A	
Comments	

Web Address	Phone
Email 2 Contact	
User Name	
Psw:	Fax
Q&A	
Comments	

Web Address	Phone
Email 2 Contact	
User Name	
Psw:	Fax
Q&A	
Comments	

Password Diary

SUBJECT

Web Address	Phone
Email 2 Contact	
User Name	
Psw	Fax
Q&A	
Comments	
Web Address	Phone
Email 2 Contact	
User Name	
Psw	Fax
Q&A	
Comments	
Web Address	Phone
Email 2 Contact	
User Name	
Psw	Fax
Q&A	
Comments	
Web Address	Phone
Email 2 Contact	
User Name	
Psw	Fax
Q&A	
Comments	
Web Address	Phone
Email 2 Contact	
User Name	
Psw	Fax
Q&A	
Comments	

N

Password Diary

SUBJECT

Web Address	Phone
Email 2 Contact	
User Name	
Psw:	Fax
Q&A	
Comments	

Web Address	Phone
Email 2 Contact	
User Name	
Psw:	Fax
Q&A	
Comments	

N

Web Address	Phone
Email 2 Contact	
User Name	
Psw:	Fax
Q&A	
Comments	

Web Address	Phone
Email 2 Contact	
User Name	
Psw:	Fax
Q&A	
Comments	

Web Address	Phone
Email 2 Contact	
User Name	
Psw:	Fax
Q&A	
Comments	

Password Diary

SUBJECT

Web Address	Phone
Email 2 Contact	
User Name	
Psw	Fax
Q&A	
Comments	

Web Address	Phone
Email 2 Contact	
User Name	
Psw	Fax
Q&A	
Comments	

N

Web Address	Phone
Email 2 Contact	
User Name	
Psw	Fax
Q&A	
Comments	

Web Address	Phone
Email 2 Contact	
User Name	
Psw	Fax
Q&A	
Comments	

Web Address	Phone
Email 2 Contact	
User Name	
Psw	Fax
Q&A	
Comments	

Password Diary

SUBJECT

Web Address	Phone

Email 2 Contact

User Name

Psw:	Fax

Q&A

Comments

Web Address	Phone

Email 2 Contact

User Name

Psw:	Fax

Q&A

Comments

Web Address	Phone

Email 2 Contact

User Name

Psw:	Fax

Q&A

Comments

Web Address	Phone

Email 2 Contact

User Name

Psw:	Fax

Q&A

Comments

Web Address	Phone

Email 2 Contact

User Name

Psw:	Fax

Q&A

Comments

Password Diary

SUBJECT

Web Address	Phone
Email 2 Contact	
User Name	
Psw:	Fax
Q&A	
Comments	

Web Address	Phone
Email 2 Contact	
User Name	
Psw:	Fax
Q&A	
Comments	

Web Address	Phone
Email 2 Contact	
User Name	
Psw:	Fax
Q&A	
Comments	

Web Address	Phone
Email 2 Contact	
User Name	
Psw:	Fax
Q&A	
Comments	

Web Address	Phone
Email 2 Contact	
User Name	
Psw:	Fax
Q&A	
Comments	

Password Diary

SUBJECT

Web Address	Phone

Email 2 Contact

User Name

Psw:	Fax

Q&A

Comments

Web Address	Phone

Email 2 Contact

User Name

Psw:	Fax

Q&A

Comments

Web Address	Phone

O Email 2 Contact

User Name

Psw:	Fax

Q&A

Comments

Web Address	Phone

Email 2 Contact

User Name

Psw:	Fax

Q&A

Comments

Web Address	Phone

Email 2 Contact

User Name

Psw:	Fax

Q&A

Comments

Password Diary

SUBJECT

Web Address	Phone
Email 2 Contact	
User Name	
Psw:	Fax
Q&A	
Comments	

Web Address	Phone
Email 2 Contact	
User Name	
Psw:	Fax
Q&A	
Comments	

Web Address	Phone
Email 2 Contact	
User Name	
Psw:	Fax
Q&A	
Comments	

O

Web Address	Phone
Email 2 Contact	
User Name	
Psw:	Fax
Q&A	
Comments	

Web Address	Phone
Email 2 Contact	
User Name	
Psw:	Fax
Q&A	
Comments	

Password Diary

SUBJECT

Web Address	Phone
Email 2 Contact	
User Name	
Psw:	Fax
Q&A	
Comments	

Web Address	Phone
Email 2 Contact	
User Name	
Psw:	Fax
Q&A	
Comments	

Web Address	Phone
Email 2 Contact	
User Name	
Psw:	Fax
Q&A	
Comments	

Web Address	Phone
Email 2 Contact	
User Name	
Psw:	Fax
Q&A	
Comments	

Web Address	Phone
Email 2 Contact	
User Name	
Psw:	Fax
Q&A	
Comments	

Password Diary

SUBJECT

Web Address	Phone
Email 2 Contact	
User Name	
Psw	Fax
Q&A	
Comments	

Web Address	Phone
Email 2 Contact	
User Name	
Psw	Fax
Q&A	
Comments	

Web Address	Phone
Email 2 Contact	
User Name	
Psw	Fax
Q&A	
Comments	

Web Address	Phone
Email 2 Contact	
User Name	
Psw	Fax
Q&A	
Comments	

Web Address	Phone
Email 2 Contact	
User Name	
Psw	Fax
Q&A	
Comments	

Password Diary

SUBJECT

Web Address	Phone
Email 2 Contact	
User Name	
Psw:	Fax
Q&A	
Comments	

Web Address	Phone
Email 2 Contact	
User Name	
Psw:	Fax
Q&A	
Comments	

Web Address	Phone
Email 2 Contact	
User Name	
Psw:	Fax
Q&A	
Comments	

Web Address	Phone
Email 2 Contact	
User Name	
Psw:	Fax
Q&A	
Comments	

Web Address	Phone
Email 2 Contact	
User Name	
Psw:	Fax
Q&A	
Comments	

Password Diary

SUBJECT

Web Address	Phone
Email 2 Contact	
User Name	
Psw.	Fax
Q&A	
Comments	

Web Address	Phone
Email 2 Contact	
User Name	
Psw.	Fax
Q&A	
Comments	

Web Address	Phone
Email 2 Contact	
User Name	
Psw.	Fax
Q&A	
Comments	

Web Address	Phone
Email 2 Contact	
User Name	
Psw.	Fax
Q&A	
Comments	

Web Address	Phone
Email 2 Contact	
User Name	
Psw.	Fax
Q&A	
Comments	

P

Password Diary

SUBJECT

Web Address	Phone
Email 2 Contact	
User Name	
Psw	Fax
Q&A	
Comments	

Web Address	Phone
Email 2 Contact	
User Name	
Psw	Fax
Q&A	
Comments	

Web Address	Phone
Email 2 Contact	
User Name	
Psw	Fax
Q&A	
Comments	

Web Address	Phone
Email 2 Contact	
User Name	
Psw	Fax
Q&A	
Comments	

Web Address	Phone
Email 2 Contact	
User Name	
Psw	Fax
Q&A	
Comments	

Password Diary

SUBJECT

Web Address	Phone
Email 2 Contact	
User Name	
Psw:	Fax
Q&A	
Comments	

Web Address	Phone
Email 2 Contact	
User Name	
Psw:	Fax
Q&A	
Comments	

Web Address	Phone
Email 2 Contact	
User Name	
Psw:	Fax
Q&A	
Comments	

P

Web Address	Phone
Email 2 Contact	
User Name	
Psw:	Fax
Q&A	
Comments	

Web Address	Phone
Email 2 Contact	
User Name	
Psw:	Fax
Q&A	
Comments	

Password Diary

SUBJECT

Web Address	Phone
Email 2 Contact	
User Name	
Psw:	Fax
Q&A	
Comments	

Web Address	Phone
Email 2 Contact	
User Name	
Psw:	Fax
Q&A	
Comments	

Web Address	Phone
Email 2 Contact	
User Name	
Psw:	Fax
Q&A	
Comments	

Web Address	Phone
Email 2 Contact	
User Name	
Psw:	Fax
Q&A	
Comments	

Web Address	Phone
Email 2 Contact	
User Name	
Psw:	Fax
Q&A	
Comments	

Password Diary

SUBJECT

Web Address	Phone
Email 2 Contact	
User Name	
Psw	Fax
Q&A	
Comments	
Web Address	Phone
Email 2 Contact	
User Name	
Psw	Fax
Q&A	
Comments	
Web Address	Phone
Email 2 Contact	
User Name	
Psw	Fax
Q&A	
Comments	
Web Address	Phone
Email 2 Contact	
User Name	
Psw	Fax
Q&A	
Comments	
Web Address	Phone
Email 2 Contact	
User Name	
Psw	Fax
Q&A	
Comments	

P

Password Diary

SUBJECT

Web Address	Phone
Email 2 Contact	
User Name	
Psw:	Fax
Q&A	
Comments	

Web Address	Phone
Email 2 Contact	
User Name	
Psw:	Fax
Q&A	
Comments	

Web Address	Phone
Email 2 Contact	
User Name	
Psw:	Fax
Q&A	
Comments	

Web Address	Phone
Email 2 Contact	
User Name	
Psw:	Fax
Q&A	
Comments	

Web Address	Phone
Email 2 Contact	
User Name	
Psw:	Fax
Q&A	
Comments	

Password Diary

SUBJECT

Web Address	Phone

Email 2 Contact

User Name

Psw:	Fax

Q&A

Comments

Web Address	Phone

Email 2 Contact

User Name

Psw:	Fax

Q&A

Comments

Web Address	Phone

Email 2 Contact

User Name

Psw:	Fax

Q&A

Comments

Web Address	Phone

Email 2 Contact

User Name

Psw:	Fax

Q&A

Comments

Web Address	Phone

Email 2 Contact

User Name

Psw:	Fax

Q&A

Comments

P

Password Diary

SUBJECT

Web Address	Phone
Email 2 Contact	
User Name	
Psw:	Fax
Q&A	
Comments	

Web Address	Phone
Email 2 Contact	
User Name	
Psw:	Fax
Q&A	
Comments	

Web Address	Phone
Email 2 Contact	
User Name	
Psw:	Fax
Q&A	
Comments	

Q

Web Address	Phone
Email 2 Contact	
User Name	
Psw:	Fax
Q&A	
Comments	

Web Address	Phone
Email 2 Contact	
User Name	
Psw:	Fax
Q&A	
Comments	

Password Diary

SUBJECT

Web Address	Phone

Email 2 Contact

User Name

Psw:	Fax

Q&A

Comments

Web Address	Phone

Email 2 Contact

User Name

Psw:	Fax

Q&A

Comments

Web Address	Phone

Email 2 Contact

User Name

Psw:	Fax

Q&A

Comments

Web Address	Phone

Email 2 Contact

User Name

Psw:	Fax

Q&A

Comments

Web Address	Phone

Email 2 Contact

User Name

Psw:	Fax

Q&A

Comments

Q

Password Diary

SUBJECT

Web Address	Phone
Email 2 Contact	
User Name	
Psw:	Fax
Q&A	
Comments	
Web Address	Phone
Email 2 Contact	
User Name	
Psw:	Fax
Q&A	
Comments	
Web Address	Phone
Email 2 Contact	
User Name	
Psw:	Fax
Q&A	
Comments	
Web Address	Phone
Email 2 Contact	
User Name	
Psw:	Fax
Q&A	
Comments	
Web Address	Phone
Email 2 Contact	
User Name	
Psw:	Fax
Q&A	
Comments	

Q

Password Diary

SUBJECT

Web Address	Phone
Email 2 Contact	
User Name	
Psw	Fax
Q&A	
Comments	

Web Address	Phone
Email 2 Contact	
User Name	
Psw	Fax
Q&A	
Comments	

Web Address	Phone
Email 2 Contact	
User Name	
Psw	Fax
Q&A	
Comments	

Web Address	Phone
Email 2 Contact	
User Name	
Psw	Fax
Q&A	
Comments	

Web Address	Phone
Email 2 Contact	
User Name	
Psw	Fax
Q&A	
Comments	

Password Diary

SUBJECT

Web Address	Phone
Email 2 Contact	
User Name	
Psw:	Fax
Q&A	
Comments	
Web Address	Phone
Email 2 Contact	
User Name	
Psw:	Fax
Q&A	
Comments	
Web Address	Phone
Email 2 Contact	
User Name	
Psw:	Fax
Q&A	
Comments	
Web Address	Phone
Email 2 Contact	
User Name	
Psw:	Fax
Q&A	
Comments	
Web Address	Phone
Email 2 Contact	
User Name	
Psw:	Fax
Q&A	
Comments	

Q

Password Diary

SUBJECT

Web Address	Phone
Email 2 Contact	
User Name	
Psw:	Fax
Q&A	
Comments	

Web Address	Phone
Email 2 Contact	
User Name	
Psw:	Fax
Q&A	
Comments	

Web Address	Phone
Email 2 Contact	
User Name	
Psw:	Fax
Q&A	
Comments	

Web Address	Phone
Email 2 Contact	
User Name	
Psw:	Fax
Q&A	
Comments	

Web Address	Phone
Email 2 Contact	
User Name	
Psw:	Fax
Q&A	
Comments	

Password Diary

SUBJECT

Web Address	Phone

Email 2 Contact

User Name

Psw:	Fax

Q&A

Comments

Web Address	Phone

Email 2 Contact

User Name

Psw:	Fax

Q&A

Comments

Web Address	Phone

Email 2 Contact

User Name

Q

Psw:	Fax

Q&A

Comments

Web Address	Phone

Email 2 Contact

User Name

Psw:	Fax

Q&A

Comments

Web Address	Phone

Email 2 Contact

User Name

Psw:	Fax

Q&A

Comments

Password Diary

SUBJECT

Web Address	Phone
Email 2 Contact	
User Name	
Psw.	Fax
Q&A	
Comments	
Web Address	Phone
Email 2 Contact	
User Name	
Psw.	Fax
Q&A	
Comments	
Web Address	Phone
Email 2 Contact	
User Name	
Psw.	Fax
Q&A	
Comments	
Web Address	Phone
Email 2 Contact	
User Name	
Psw.	Fax
Q&A	
Comments	
Web Address	Phone
Email 2 Contact	
User Name	
Psw.	Fax
Q&A	
Comments	

R

Password Diary

SUBJECT

Web Address	Phone
Email 2 Contact	
User Name	
Psw:	Fax
Q&A	
Comments	

Web Address	Phone
Email 2 Contact	
User Name	
Psw:	Fax
Q&A	
Comments	

Web Address	Phone
Email 2 Contact	
User Name	
Psw:	Fax
Q&A	
Comments	

R

Web Address	Phone
Email 2 Contact	
User Name	
Psw:	Fax
Q&A	
Comments	

Web Address	Phone
Email 2 Contact	
User Name	
Psw:	Fax
Q&A	
Comments	

Password Diary

SUBJECT

Web Address	Phone
Email 2 Contact	
User Name	
Psw:	Fax
Q&A	
Comments	
Web Address	Phone
Email 2 Contact	
User Name	
Psw:	Fax
Q&A	
Comments	
Web Address	Phone
Email 2 Contact	
User Name	
Psw:	Fax
Q&A	
Comments	
Web Address	Phone
Email 2 Contact	
User Name	
Psw:	Fax
Q&A	
Comments	
Web Address	Phone
Email 2 Contact	
User Name	
Psw:	Fax
Q&A	
Comments	

R

Password Diary

SUBJECT

Web Address	Phone
Email 2 Contact	
User Name	
Psw:	Fax
Q&A	
Comments	

Web Address	Phone
Email 2 Contact	
User Name	
Psw:	Fax
Q&A	
Comments	

Web Address	Phone
Email 2 Contact	
User Name	
Psw:	Fax
Q&A	
Comments	

R

Web Address	Phone
Email 2 Contact	
User Name	
Psw:	Fax
Q&A	
Comments	

Web Address	Phone
Email 2 Contact	
User Name	
Psw:	Fax
Q&A	
Comments	

Password Diary

SUBJECT

Web Address	Phone
Email 2 Contact	
User Name	
Psw:	Fax
Q&A	
Comments	

Web Address	Phone
Email 2 Contact	
User Name	
Psw:	Fax
Q&A	
Comments	

Web Address	Phone
Email 2 Contact	
User Name	
Psw:	Fax
Q&A	
Comments	

R

Web Address	Phone
Email 2 Contact	
User Name	
Psw:	Fax
Q&A	
Comments	

Web Address	Phone
Email 2 Contact	
User Name	
Psw:	Fax
Q&A	
Comments	

Password Diary

SUBJECT

Web Address	Phone
Email 2 Contact	
User Name	
Psw:	Fax
Q&A	
Comments	|ощ
Web Address	Phone
Email 2 Contact	
User Name	
Psw:	Fax
Q&A	
Comments	

Web Address	Phone
Email 2 Contact	
User Name	
Psw:	Fax
Q&A	
Comments	

Web Address	Phone
Email 2 Contact	
User Name	
Psw:	Fax
Q&A	
Comments	

Web Address	Phone
Email 2 Contact	
User Name	
Psw:	Fax
Q&A	
Comments	

R

Password Diary

SUBJECT

Web Address	Phone

Email 2 Contact

User Name

Psw:	Fax

Q&A

Comments

Web Address	Phone

Email 2 Contact

User Name

Psw:	Fax

Q&A

Comments

Web Address	Phone

Email 2 Contact

User Name

Psw:	Fax

Q&A

Comments

Web Address	Phone

Email 2 Contact

User Name

Psw:	Fax

Q&A

Comments

Web Address	Phone

Email 2 Contact

User Name

Psw:	Fax

Q&A

Comments

R

Password Diary

SUBJECT

Web Address	Phone
Email 2 Contact	
User Name	
Psw:	Fax
Q&A	
Comments	

Web Address	Phone
Email 2 Contact	
User Name	
Psw:	Fax
Q&A	
Comments	

S

Web Address	Phone
Email 2 Contact	
User Name	
Psw:	Fax
Q&A	
Comments	

Web Address	Phone
Email 2 Contact	
User Name	
Psw:	Fax
Q&A	
Comments	

Web Address	Phone
Email 2 Contact	
User Name	
Psw:	Fax
Q&A	
Comments	

Password Diary

SUBJECT

Web Address	Phone

Email 2 Contact

User Name

Psw	Fax

Q&A

Comments

Web Address	Phone

Email 2 Contact

User Name

Psw	Fax

Q&A

Comments

Web Address	Phone

Email 2 Contact

User Name

Psw	Fax

Q&A

Comments

S

Web Address	Phone

Email 2 Contact

User Name

Psw	Fax

Q&A

Comments

Web Address	Phone

Email 2 Contact

User Name

Psw	Fax

Q&A

Comments

Password Diary

SUBJECT

Web Address	Phone
Email 2 Contact	
User Name	
Psw:	Fax
Q&A	
Comments	

Web Address	Phone
Email 2 Contact	
User Name	
Psw:	Fax
Q&A	
Comments	

Web Address	Phone
Email 2 Contact	
User Name	
Psw:	Fax
Q&A	
Comments	

S

Web Address	Phone
Email 2 Contact	
User Name	
Psw:	Fax
Q&A	
Comments	

Web Address	Phone
Email 2 Contact	
User Name	
Psw:	Fax
Q&A	
Comments	

Password Diary

SUBJECT

Web Address	Phone

| Email 2 Contact | |

| User Name | |

Psw:	Fax

| Q&A | |

| Comments | |

Web Address	Phone

| Email 2 Contact | |

| User Name | |

Psw:	Fax

| Q&A | |

| Comments | |

Web Address	Phone

| Email 2 Contact | |

| User Name | |

Psw:	Fax

| Q&A | |

| Comments | |

S

Web Address	Phone

| Email 2 Contact | |

| User Name | |

Psw:	Fax

| Q&A | |

| Comments | |

Web Address	Phone

| Email 2 Contact | |

| User Name | |

Psw:	Fax

| Q&A | |

| Comments | |

Password Diary

SUBJECT

| Web Address | Phone |
|---|---|//
Email 2 Contact	
User Name	
Psw:	Fax
Q&A	
Comments	
Web Address	Phone
Email 2 Contact	
User Name	
Psw:	Fax
Q&A	
Comments	
Web Address	Phone
Email 2 Contact	
User Name	
Psw:	Fax
Q&A	
Comments	
Web Address	Phone
Email 2 Contact	
User Name	
Psw:	Fax
Q&A	
Comments	
Web Address	Phone
Email 2 Contact	
User Name	
Psw:	Fax
Q&A	
Comments	

Password Diary

SUBJECT

Web Address	Phone
Email 2 Contact	
User Name	
Psw:	Fax
Q&A	
Comments	
Web Address	Phone
Email 2 Contact	
User Name	
Psw:	Fax
Q&A	
Comments	
Web Address	Phone
Email 2 Contact	
User Name	
Psw:	Fax
Q&A	
Comments	
Web Address	Phone
Email 2 Contact	
User Name	
Psw:	Fax
Q&A	
Comments	
Web Address	Phone
Email 2 Contact	
User Name	
Psw:	Fax
Q&A	
Comments	

S

Password Diary

SUBJECT

Web Address	Phone
Email 2 Contact	
User Name	
Psw:	Fax
Q&A	
Comments	
Web Address	Phone
Email 2 Contact	
User Name	
Psw:	Fax
Q&A	
Comments	
Web Address	Phone
Email 2 Contact	
User Name	
Psw:	Fax
Q&A	
Comments	
Web Address	Phone
Email 2 Contact	
User Name	
Psw:	Fax
Q&A	
Comments	
Web Address	Phone
Email 2 Contact	
User Name	
Psw:	Fax
Q&A	
Comments	

S

Password Diary

SUBJECT

Web Address	Phone
Email 2 Contact	
User Name	
Psw	Fax
Q&A	
Comments	
Web Address	Phone
Email 2 Contact	
User Name	
Psw	Fax
Q&A	
Comments	
Web Address	Phone
Email 2 Contact	
User Name	
Psw	Fax
Q&A	
Comments	
Web Address	Phone
Email 2 Contact	
User Name	
Psw	Fax
Q&A	
Comments	
Web Address	Phone
Email 2 Contact	
User Name	
Psw	Fax
Q&A	
Comments	

T

Password Diary

SUBJECT

Web Address	Phone
Email 2 Contact	
User Name	
Psw:	Fax
Q&A	
Comments	

Web Address	Phone
Email 2 Contact	
User Name	
Psw:	Fax
Q&A	
Comments	

Web Address	Phone
Email 2 Contact	
User Name	
Psw:	Fax
Q&A	
Comments	

T

Web Address	Phone
Email 2 Contact	
User Name	
Psw:	Fax
Q&A	
Comments	

Web Address	Phone
Email 2 Contact	
User Name	
Psw:	Fax
Q&A	
Comments	

Password Diary

SUBJECT

Web Address	Phone
Email 2 Contact	
User Name	
Psw:	Fax
Q&A	
Comments	

Web Address	Phone
Email 2 Contact	
User Name	
Psw:	Fax
Q&A	
Comments	

Web Address	Phone
Email 2 Contact	
User Name	
Psw:	Fax
Q&A	
Comments	

Web Address	Phone
Email 2 Contact	
User Name	
Psw:	Fax
Q&A	
Comments	

Web Address	Phone
Email 2 Contact	
User Name	
Psw:	Fax
Q&A	
Comments	

T

Password Diary

SUBJECT

Web Address	Phone

Email 2 Contact

User Name

Psw:	Fax

Q&A

Comments

Web Address	Phone

Email 2 Contact

User Name

Psw:	Fax

Q&A

Comments

Web Address	Phone

Email 2 Contact

User Name

Psw:	Fax

Q&A

Comments

T

Web Address	Phone

Email 2 Contact

User Name

Psw:	Fax

Q&A

Comments

Web Address	Phone

Email 2 Contact

User Name

Psw:	Fax

Q&A

Comments

Password Diary

SUBJECT

Web Address	Phone
Email 2 Contact	
User Name	
Psw:	Fax
Q&A	
Comments	

Web Address	Phone
Email 2 Contact	
User Name	
Psw:	Fax
Q&A	
Comments	

Web Address	Phone
Email 2 Contact	
User Name	
Psw:	Fax
Q&A	
Comments	

Web Address	Phone
Email 2 Contact	
User Name	
Psw:	Fax
Q&A	
Comments	

T

Web Address	Phone
Email 2 Contact	
User Name	
Psw:	Fax
Q&A	
Comments	

Password Diary

SUBJECT

Web Address	Phone
Email 2 Contact	
User Name	
Psw:	Fax
Q&A	
Comments	

Web Address	Phone
Email 2 Contact	
User Name	
Psw:	Fax
Q&A	
Comments	

Web Address	Phone
Email 2 Contact	
User Name	
Psw:	Fax
Q&A	
Comments	

T

Web Address	Phone
Email 2 Contact	
User Name	
Psw:	Fax
Q&A	
Comments	

Web Address	Phone
Email 2 Contact	
User Name	
Psw:	Fax
Q&A	
Comments	

Password Diary

SUBJECT

Web Address	Phone

Email 2 Contact

User Name

Psw	Fax

Q&A

Comments

Web Address	Phone

Email 2 Contact

User Name

Psw	Fax

Q&A

Comments

Web Address	Phone

Email 2 Contact

User Name

Psw	Fax

Q&A

Comments

Web Address	Phone

Email 2 Contact

User Name

Psw	Fax

Q&A

Comments

Web Address	Phone

Email 2 Contact

User Name

Psw	Fax

Q&A

Comments

Password Diary

SUBJECT

Web Address	Phone
Email 2 Contact	
User Name	
Psw:	Fax
Q&A	
Comments	

Web Address	Phone
Email 2 Contact	
User Name	
Psw:	Fax
Q&A	
Comments	

Web Address	Phone
Email 2 Contact	
User Name	
Psw:	Fax
Q&A	
Comments	

U

Web Address	Phone
Email 2 Contact	
User Name	
Psw:	Fax
Q&A	
Comments	

Web Address	Phone
Email 2 Contact	
User Name	
Psw:	Fax
Q&A	
Comments	

Password Diary

SUBJECT

Web Address	Phone
Email 2 Contact	
User Name	
Psw	Fax
Q&A	
Comments	

Web Address	Phone
Email 2 Contact	
User Name	
Psw	Fax
Q&A	
Comments	

Web Address	Phone
Email 2 Contact	
User Name	
Psw	Fax
Q&A	
Comments	

Web Address	Phone
Email 2 Contact	
User Name	
Psw	Fax
Q&A	
Comments	

U

Web Address	Phone
Email 2 Contact	
User Name	
Psw	Fax
Q&A	
Comments	

Password Diary

SUBJECT

Web Address	Phone

Email 2 Contact

User Name

Psw:	Fax

Q&A

Comments

Web Address	Phone

Email 2 Contact

User Name

Psw:	Fax

Q&A

Comments

Web Address	Phone

Email 2 Contact

User Name

Psw:	Fax

Q&A

Comments

Web Address	Phone

U Email 2 Contact

User Name

Psw:	Fax

Q&A

Comments

Web Address	Phone

Email 2 Contact

User Name

Psw:	Fax

Q&A

Comments

Password Diary

SUBJECT

Web Address	Phone
Email 2 Contact	
User Name	
Psw:	Fax
Q&A	
Comments	

Web Address	Phone
Email 2 Contact	
User Name	
Psw:	Fax
Q&A	
Comments	

Web Address	Phone
Email 2 Contact	
User Name	
Psw:	Fax
Q&A	
Comments	

Web Address	Phone
Email 2 Contact	
User Name	
Psw:	Fax
Q&A	
Comments	

Web Address	Phone
Email 2 Contact	
User Name	
Psw:	Fax
Q&A	
Comments	

U

Password Diary

SUBJECT

Web Address	Phone
Email 2 Contact	
User Name	
Psw:	Fax
Q&A	
Comments	

Web Address	Phone
Email 2 Contact	
User Name	
Psw:	Fax
Q&A	
Comments	

Web Address	Phone
Email 2 Contact	
User Name	
Psw:	Fax
Q&A	
Comments	

U

Web Address	Phone
Email 2 Contact	
User Name	
Psw:	Fax
Q&A	
Comments	

Web Address	Phone
Email 2 Contact	
User Name	
Psw:	Fax
Q&A	
Comments	

Password Diary

SUBJECT

Web Address	Phone
Email 2 Contact	
User Name	
Psw	Fax
Q&A	
Comments	
Web Address	Phone
Email 2 Contact	
User Name	
Psw	Fax
Q&A	
Comments	
Web Address	Phone
Email 2 Contact	
User Name	
Psw	Fax
Q&A	
Comments	
Web Address	Phone
Email 2 Contact	
User Name	
Psw	Fax
Q&A	
Comments	
Web Address	Phone
Email 2 Contact	
User Name	
Psw	Fax
Q&A	
Comments	

U

Password Diary

SUBJECT

Web Address	Phone
Email 2 Contact	
User Name	
Psw:	Fax
Q&A	
Comments	

Web Address	Phone
Email 2 Contact	
User Name	
Psw:	Fax
Q&A	
Comments	

Web Address	Phone
Email 2 Contact	
User Name	
Psw:	Fax
Q&A	
Comments	

U

Web Address	Phone
Email 2 Contact	
User Name	
Psw:	Fax
Q&A	
Comments	

Web Address	Phone
Email 2 Contact	
User Name	
Psw:	Fax
Q&A	
Comments	

Password Diary

SUBJECT

Web Address	Phone
Email 2 Contact	
User Name	
Psw	Fax
Q&A	
Comments	

Web Address	Phone
Email 2 Contact	
User Name	
Psw	Fax
Q&A	
Comments	

Web Address	Phone
Email 2 Contact	
User Name	
Psw	Fax
Q&A	
Comments	

Web Address	Phone
Email 2 Contact	
User Name	
Psw	Fax
Q&A	
Comments	

Web Address	Phone
Email 2 Contact	
User Name	
Psw	Fax
Q&A	
Comments	

V

Password Diary

SUBJECT

Web Address	Phone
Email 2 Contact	
User Name	
Psw:	Fax
Q&A	
Comments	

Web Address	Phone
Email 2 Contact	
User Name	
Psw:	Fax
Q&A	
Comments	

Web Address	Phone
Email 2 Contact	
User Name	
Psw:	Fax
Q&A	
Comments	

V

Web Address	Phone
Email 2 Contact	
User Name	
Psw:	Fax
Q&A	
Comments	

Web Address	Phone
Email 2 Contact	
User Name	
Psw:	Fax
Q&A	
Comments	

Password Diary

SUBJECT

Web Address	Phone

Email 2 Contact

User Name

Psw:	Fax

Q&A

Comments

Web Address	Phone

Email 2 Contact

User Name

Psw:	Fax

Q&A

Comments

Web Address	Phone

Email 2 Contact

User Name

Psw:	Fax

Q&A

Comments

Web Address	Phone

Email 2 Contact

User Name

Psw:	Fax

Q&A

Comments

Web Address	Phone

Email 2 Contact

User Name

Psw:	Fax

Q&A

Comments

V

Password Diary

SUBJECT

Web Address	Phone
Email 2 Contact	
User Name	
Psw:	Fax
Q&A	
Comments	

Web Address	Phone
Email 2 Contact	
User Name	
Psw:	Fax
Q&A	
Comments	

Web Address	Phone
Email 2 Contact	
User Name	
Psw:	Fax
Q&A	
Comments	

V

Web Address	Phone
Email 2 Contact	
User Name	
Psw:	Fax
Q&A	
Comments	

Web Address	Phone
Email 2 Contact	
User Name	
Psw:	Fax
Q&A	
Comments	

Password Diary

SUBJECT

Web Address	Phone
Email 2 Contact	
User Name	
Psw	Fax
Q&A	
Comments	
Web Address	Phone
Email 2 Contact	
User Name	
Psw	Fax
Q&A	
Comments	
Web Address	Phone
Email 2 Contact	
User Name	
Psw	Fax
Q&A	
Comments	
Web Address	Phone
Email 2 Contact	
User Name	
Psw	Fax
Q&A	
Comments	
Web Address	Phone
Email 2 Contact	
User Name	
Psw	Fax
Q&A	
Comments	

V

Password Diary

SUBJECT

Web Address	Phone
Email 2 Contact	
User Name	
Psw:	Fax
Q&A	
Comments	

Web Address	Phone
Email 2 Contact	
User Name	
Psw:	Fax
Q&A	
Comments	

Web Address	Phone
Email 2 Contact	
User Name	
Psw:	Fax
Q&A	
Comments	

V

Web Address	Phone
Email 2 Contact	
User Name	
Psw:	Fax
Q&A	
Comments	

Web Address	Phone
Email 2 Contact	
User Name	
Psw	Fax
Q&A	
Comments	

Password Diary

SUBJECT

Web Address	Phone
Email 2 Contact	
User Name	
Psw:	Fax
Q&A	
Comments	
Web Address	Phone
Email 2 Contact	
User Name	
Psw:	Fax
Q&A	
Comments	
Web Address	Phone
Email 2 Contact	
User Name	
Psw:	Fax
Q&A	
Comments	
Web Address	Phone
Email 2 Contact	
User Name	
Psw:	Fax
Q&A	
Comments	
Web Address	Phone
Email 2 Contact	
User Name	
Psw:	Fax
Q&A	
Comments	

W

Password Diary

SUBJECT

Web Address	Phone
Email 2 Contact	
User Name	
Psw:	Fax
Q&A	
Comments	

Web Address	Phone
Email 2 Contact	
User Name	
Psw:	Fax
Q&A	
Comments	

Web Address	Phone
Email 2 Contact	
User Name	
Psw:	Fax
Q&A	
Comments	

W

Web Address	Phone
Email 2 Contact	
User Name	
Psw:	Fax
Q&A	
Comments	

Web Address	Phone
Email 2 Contact	
User Name	
Psw:	Fax
Q&A	
Comments	

Password Diary

SUBJECT

Web Address	Phone
Email 2 Contact	
User Name	
Psw:	Fax
Q&A	
Comments	
Web Address	Phone
Email 2 Contact	
User Name	
Psw:	Fax
Q&A	
Comments	
Web Address	Phone
Email 2 Contact	
User Name	
Psw:	Fax
Q&A	
Comments	
Web Address	Phone
Email 2 Contact	
User Name	
Psw:	Fax
Q&A	
Comments	
Web Address	Phone
Email 2 Contact	
User Name	
Psw:	Fax
Q&A	
Comments	

Password Diary

SUBJECT

Web Address	Phone
Email 2 Contact	
User Name	
Psw:	Fax
Q&A	
Comments	

Web Address	Phone
Email 2 Contact	
User Name	
Psw:	Fax
Q&A	
Comments	

Web Address	Phone
Email 2 Contact	
User Name	
Psw:	Fax
Q&A	
Comments	

Web Address	Phone
Email 2 Contact	
User Name	
Psw:	Fax
Q&A	
Comments	

Web Address	Phone
Email 2 Contact	
User Name	
Psw:	Fax
Q&A	
Comments	

W

Password Diary

SUBJECT

Web Address	Phone
Email 2 Contact	
User Name	
Psw	Fax
Q&A	
Comments	
Web Address	Phone
Email 2 Contact	
User Name	
Psw	Fax
Q&A	
Comments	
Web Address	Phone
Email 2 Contact	
User Name	
Psw	Fax
Q&A	
Comments	
Web Address	Phone
Email 2 Contact	
User Name	
Psw	Fax
Q&A	
Comments	
Web Address	Phone
Email 2 Contact	
User Name	
Psw	Fax
Q&A	
Comments	

W

Password Diary

SUBJECT

Web Address	Phone
Email 2 Contact	
User Name	
Psw:	Fax
Q&A	
Comments	

Web Address	Phone
Email 2 Contact	
User Name	
Psw:	Fax
Q&A	
Comments	

Web Address	Phone
Email 2 Contact	
User Name	
Psw:	Fax
Q&A	
Comments	

Web Address	Phone
Email 2 Contact	
User Name	
Psw:	Fax
Q&A	
Comments	

W

Web Address	Phone
Email 2 Contact	
User Name	
Psw:	Fax
Q&A	
Comments	

Password Diary

SUBJECT

Web Address	Phone
Email 2 Contact	
User Name	
Psw:	Fax
Q&A	
Comments	

Web Address	Phone
Email 2 Contact	
User Name	
Psw:	Fax
Q&A	
Comments	

Web Address	Phone
Email 2 Contact	
User Name	
Psw:	Fax
Q&A	
Comments	

Web Address	Phone
Email 2 Contact	
User Name	
Psw:	Fax
Q&A	X
Comments	

Web Address	Phone
Email 2 Contact	
User Name	
Psw:	Fax
Q&A	
Comments	

Password Diary

SUBJECT

Web Address	Phone
Email 2 Contact	
User Name	
Psw:	Fax
Q&A	
Comments	
Web Address	Phone
Email 2 Contact	
User Name	
Psw:	Fax
Q&A	
Comments	
Web Address	Phone
Email 2 Contact	
User Name	
Psw:	Fax
Q&A	
Comments	
Web Address	Phone
Email 2 Contact	
User Name	
Psw:	Fax
Q&A	
Comments	
Web Address	Phone
Email 2 Contact	
User Name	
Psw:	Fax
Q&A	
Comments	

Password Diary

SUBJECT

Web Address	Phone
Email 2 Contact	
User Name	
Psw.	Fax
Q&A	
Comments	

Web Address	Phone
Email 2 Contact	
User Name	
Psw.	Fax
Q&A	
Comments	

Web Address	Phone
Email 2 Contact	
User Name	
Psw.	Fax
Q&A	
Comments	

Web Address	Phone
Email 2 Contact	
User Name	
Psw.	Fax
Q&A	
Comments	

Web Address	Phone
Email 2 Contact	
User Name	
Psw.	Fax
Q&A	
Comments	

X

Password Diary

SUBJECT

Web Address	Phone
Email 2 Contact	
User Name	
Psw:	Fax
Q&A	
Comments	

Web Address	Phone
Email 2 Contact	
User Name	
Psw:	Fax
Q&A	
Comments	

Web Address	Phone
Email 2 Contact	
User Name	
Psw:	Fax
Q&A	
Comments	

Web Address	Phone
Email 2 Contact	
User Name	
Psw:	Fax
Q&A	
Comments	

Web Address	Phone
Email 2 Contact	
User Name	
Psw:	Fax
Q&A	
Comments	

X

Password Diary

SUBJECT

Web Address	Phone
Email 2 Contact	
User Name	
Psw	Fax
Q&A	
Comments	
Web Address	Phone
Email 2 Contact	
User Name	
Psw	Fax
Q&A	
Comments	
Web Address	Phone
Email 2 Contact	
User Name	
Psw	Fax
Q&A	
Comments	
Web Address	Phone
Email 2 Contact	
User Name	
Psw	Fax
Q&A	
Comments	
Web Address	Phone
Email 2 Contact	
User Name	
Psw	Fax
Q&A	
Comments	

Password Diary

SUBJECT

Web Address	Phone
Email 2 Contact	
User Name	
Psw:	Fax
Q&A	
Comments	
Web Address	Phone
Email 2 Contact	
User Name	
Psw:	Fax
Q&A	
Comments	
Web Address	Phone
Email 2 Contact	
User Name	
Psw:	Fax
Q&A	
Comments	
Web Address	Phone
Email 2 Contact	
User Name	
Psw:	Fax
Q&A	
Comments	
Web Address	Phone
Email 2 Contact	
User Name	
Psw:	Fax
Q&A	
Comments	

Password Diary

SUBJECT

Web Address	Phone
Email 2 Contact	
User Name	
Psw:	Fax
Q&A	
Comments	

Web Address	Phone
Email 2 Contact	
User Name	
Psw:	Fax
Q&A	
Comments	

Web Address	Phone
Email 2 Contact	
User Name	
Psw:	Fax
Q&A	
Comments	

Web Address	Phone
Email 2 Contact	
User Name	
Psw:	Fax
Q&A	
Comments	Y

Web Address	Phone
Email 2 Contact	
User Name	
Psw:	Fax
Q&A	
Comments	

Password Diary

SUBJECT

Web Address	Phone
Email 2 Contact	
User Name	
Psw:	Fax
Q&A	
Comments	
Web Address	Phone
Email 2 Contact	
User Name	
Psw:	Fax
Q&A	
Comments	
Web Address	Phone
Email 2 Contact	
User Name	
Psw:	Fax
Q&A	
Comments	
Web Address	Phone
Email 2 Contact	
User Name	
Psw:	Fax
Q&A	

Y Comments

Web Address	Phone
Email 2 Contact	
User Name	
Psw:	Fax
Q&A	
Comments	

Password Diary

SUBJECT

Web Address	Phone
Email 2 Contact	
User Name	
Psw:	Fax
Q&A	
Comments	

Web Address	Phone
Email 2 Contact	
User Name	
Psw:	Fax
Q&A	
Comments	

Web Address	Phone
Email 2 Contact	
User Name	
Psw:	Fax
Q&A	
Comments	

Web Address	Phone
Email 2 Contact	
User Name	
Psw:	Fax
Q&A	
Comments	

Y

Web Address	Phone
Email 2 Contact	
User Name	
Psw:	Fax
Q&A	
Comments	

Password Diary

SUBJECT

Web Address	Phone
Email 2 Contact	
User Name	
Psw:	Fax
Q&A	
Comments	

Web Address	Phone
Email 2 Contact	
User Name	
Psw:	Fax
Q&A	
Comments	

Web Address	Phone
Email 2 Contact	
User Name	
Psw:	Fax
Q&A	
Comments	

Web Address	Phone
Email 2 Contact	
User Name	
Psw:	Fax
Q&A	

Y Comments

Web Address	Phone
Email 2 Contact	
User Name	
Psw:	Fax
Q&A	
Comments	

Password Diary

SUBJECT

Web Address	Phone
Email 2 Contact	
User Name	
Psw	Fax
Q&A	
Comments	

Web Address	Phone
Email 2 Contact	
User Name	
Psw	Fax
Q&A	
Comments	

Web Address	Phone
Email 2 Contact	
User Name	
Psw	Fax
Q&A	
Comments	

Web Address	Phone
Email 2 Contact	
User Name	
Psw	Fax
Q&A	
Comments	

Y

Web Address	Phone
Email 2 Contact	
User Name	
Psw	Fax
Q&A	
Comments	

Password Diary

SUBJECT

Web Address	Phone
Email 2 Contact	
User Name	
Psw:	Fax
Q&A	
Comments	

Web Address	Phone
Email 2 Contact	
User Name	
Psw:	Fax
Q&A	
Comments	

Web Address	Phone
Email 2 Contact	
User Name	
Psw:	Fax
Q&A	
Comments	

Web Address	Phone
Email 2 Contact	
User Name	
Psw:	Fax
Q&A	

Y Comments

Web Address	Phone
Email 2 Contact	
User Name	
Psw:	Fax
Q&A	
Comments	

Password Diary

SUBJECT

Web Address	Phone
Email 2 Contact	
User Name	
Psw:	Fax
Q&A	
Comments	

Web Address	Phone
Email 2 Contact	
User Name	
Psw:	Fax
Q&A	
Comments	

Web Address	Phone
Email 2 Contact	
User Name	
Psw:	Fax
Q&A	
Comments	

Web Address	Phone
Email 2 Contact	
User Name	
Psw:	Fax
Q&A	
Comments	

Z

Web Address	Phone
Email 2 Contact	
User Name	
Psw:	Fax
Q&A	
Comments	

Password Diary

SUBJECT

Web Address	Phone

Email 2 Contact

User Name

Psw:	Fax

Q&A

Comments

Web Address	Phone

Email 2 Contact

User Name

Psw	Fax

Q&A

Comments

Web Address	Phone

Email 2 Contact

User Name

Psw:	Fax

Q&A

Comments

Web Address	Phone

Email 2 Contact

User Name

Psw:	Fax

Q&A

Comments

Z

Web Address	Phone

Email 2 Contact

User Name

Psw:	Fax

Q&A

Comments

Password Diary

SUBJECT

Web Address	Phone
Email 2 Contact	
User Name	
Psw:	Fax
Q&A	
Comments	

Web Address	Phone
Email 2 Contact	
User Name	
Psw:	Fax
Q&A	
Comments	

Web Address	Phone
Email 2 Contact	
User Name	
Psw:	Fax
Q&A	
Comments	

Web Address	Phone
Email 2 Contact	
User Name	
Psw:	Fax
Q&A	
Comments	

Web Address	Phone
Email 2 Contact	
User Name	
Psw:	Fax
Q&A	
Comments	

Z

Password Diary

SUBJECT

Web Address	Phone
Email 2 Contact	
User Name	
Psw:	Fax
Q&A	
Comments	

Web Address	Phone
Email 2 Contact	
User Name	
Psw:	Fax
Q&A	
Comments	

Web Address	Phone
Email 2 Contact	
User Name	
Psw:	Fax
Q&A	
Comments	

Web Address	Phone
Email 2 Contact	
User Name	
Psw:	Fax
Q&A	
Comments	

Z

Web Address	Phone
Email 2 Contact	
User Name	
Psw:	Fax
Q&A	
Comments	

Password Diary

SUBJECT

Web Address	Phone
Email 2 Contact	
User Name	
Psw	Fax
Q&A	
Comments	
Web Address	Phone
Email 2 Contact	
User Name	
Psw	Fax
Q&A	
Comments	
Web Address	Phone
Email 2 Contact	
User Name	
Psw	Fax
Q&A	
Comments	
Web Address	Phone
Email 2 Contact	
User Name	
Psw	Fax
Q&A	
Comments	
Web Address	Phone
Email 2 Contact	
User Name	
Psw	Fax
Q&A	
Comments	

Z

Password Diary

SUBJECT

Web Address	Phone
Email 2 Contact	
User Name	
Psw:	Fax
Q&A	
Comments	

Web Address	Phone
Email 2 Contact	
User Name	
Psw:	Fax
Q&A	
Comments	

Web Address	Phone
Email 2 Contact	
User Name	
Psw:	Fax
Q&A	
Comments	

Web Address	Phone
Email 2 Contact	
User Name	
Psw:	Fax
Q&A	
Comments	

Z

Web Address	Phone
Email 2 Contact	
User Name	
Psw:	Fax
Q&A	
Comments	

Password Diary

BUSINESS NAME

Team Website	Psw
Email 1	Psw
Email 2	Psw
Email 3	Psw
Email 4	Psw
Email 5	Psw
Email 6	Psw
Email 7	Psw
Email 8	Psw
Facebook Fan Page	Psw
Blog	Psw
YouTube	Psw
Tweeter	Psw
My Space	Psw
Other	Psw
Office Ph#	Ext
Cell Ph#	

Comments

B U S

Password Diary

BUSINESS NAME

Team Website	Psw
Email 1	Psw
Email 2	Psw
Email 3	Psw
Email 4	Psw
Email 5	Psw
Email 6	Psw
Email 7	Psw
Email 8	Psw
Facebook Fan Page	Psw
Blog	Psw
YouTube	Psw
Tweeter	Psw
My Space	Psw
Other	Psw
Office Ph#	Ext
Cell Ph#	

Comments

BUS

Password Diary

BUSINESS NAME

Team Website	Psw
Email 1	Psw
Email 2	Psw
Email 3	Psw
Email 4	Psw
Email 5	Psw
Email 6	Psw
Email 7	Psw
Email 8	Psw
Facebook Fan Page	Psw
Blog	Psw
YouTube	Psw
Tweeter	Psw
My Space	Psw
Other	Psw
Office Ph#	Ext
Cell Ph#	

Comments

BUS

Password Diary

BUSINESS NAME

Team Website	Psw
Email 1	Psw
Email 2	Psw
Email 3	Psw
Email 4	Psw
Email 5	Psw
Email 6	Psw
Email 7	Psw
Email 8	Psw
Facebook Fan Page	Psw
Blog	Psw
YouTube	Psw
Tweeter	Psw
My Space	Psw
Other	Psw
Office Ph#	Ext.
Cell Ph#	

Comments

Password Diary

BUSINESS NAME

Team Website	Psw
Email 1	Psw
Email 2	Psw
Email 3	Psw
Email 4	Psw
Email 5	Psw
Email 6	Psw
Email 7	Psw
Email 8	Psw
Facebook Fan Page	Psw
Blog	Psw
YouTube	Psw
Tweeter	Psw
My Space	Psw
Other	Psw
Office Ph#	Ext.
Cell Ph#	

Comments

BUS

Password Diary

BUSINESS NAME

Team Website	Psw
Email 1	Psw
Email 2	Psw
Email 3	Psw
Email 4	Psw
Email 5	Psw
Email 6	Psw
Email 7	Psw
Email 8	Psw
Facebook Fan Page	Psw
Blog	Psw
YouTube	Psw
Tweeter	Psw
My Space	Psw
Other	Psw
Office Ph#	Ext.
Cell Ph#	

Comments

Password Diary

BUSINESS NAME

Team Website	Psw
Email 1	Psw
Email 2	Psw
Email 3	Psw
Email 4	Psw
Email 5	Psw
Email 6	Psw
Email 7	Psw
Email 8	Psw
Facebook Fan Page	Psw
Blog	Psw
YouTube	Psw
Tweeter	Psw
My Space	Psw
Other	Psw
Office Ph#	Ext.
Cell Ph#	

Comments

B U S

Password Diary

BUSINESS NAME

Team Website	Psw
Email 1	Psw
Email 2	Psw
Email 3	Psw
Email 4	Psw
Email 5	Psw
Email 6	Psw
Email 7	Psw
Email 8	Psw
Facebook Fan Page	Psw
Blog	Psw
YouTube	Psw
Tweeter	Psw
My Space	Psw
Other	Psw
Office Ph#	Ext.
Cell Ph#	

B U S

Comments

Password Diary

WEBSITE

Domain Name		IP
Reg. Date	Exp. Date	
Adm Ph.		
Email	Psw	

Tech Contact Details Name:

Email		Phone

Registrar Name:

Server Details:

1

2

Hosting	Date

User Name:

Psw:

IP:

Name Server

1

2

Comments

Password Diary

WEBSITE

Domain Name		IP	
Reg. Date	Exp. Date		

Adm Ph.

Email	Psw

Tech Contact Details Name:

Email	Phone

Registrar Name:

Server Details:

1

2

Hosting	Date

User Name:

Psw.

IP:

Name Server

1

2

Comments

Password Diary

WEBSITE

Domain Name		IP	
Reg. Date	Exp. Date		

Adm Ph.

Email	Psw

Tech Contact Details Name:

Email	Phone

Registrar Name:

Server Details:

1.

2.

Hosting	Date

User Name:

Psw

IP

Name Server

1.

2.

Comments

W S

Password Diary

WEBSITE

Domain Name	IP
Reg. Date	Exp. Date

Adm Ph.

Email	Psw

Tech Contact Details Name.

Email	Phone

Registrar Name.

Server Details:

1

2

Hosting	Date

User Name.

Psw:

IP:

Name Server

1

2

Comments

Password Diary

WEBSITE

Domain Name		IP

Reg. Date	Exp. Date	

Adm Ph.

Email		Psw

Tech Contact Details Name:

Email		Phone

Registrar Name

Server Details

1

2

Hosting		Date

User Name

Psw.

IP

Name Server

1

2

Comments

W
S

Password Diary

WEBSITE

Domain Name		IP

Reg. Date	Exp. Date

Adm Ph.

Email	Psw

Tech Contact Details Name

Email	Phone

Registrar Name:

Server Details:

1

2

Hosting	Date

User Name:

Psw:

IP:

Name Server

1

2

Comments

Password Diary

WEBSITE

Domain Name		IP
Reg. Date	Exp. Date	

Adm Ph.

Email	Psw

Tech Contact Details Name:

Email	Phone

Registrar Name:

Server Details:

1.

2.

Hosting	Date

User Name:

Psw:

IP:

Name Server

1.

2.

Comments

Password Diary

WEBSITE

Domain Name		IP	
Reg. Date		Exp. Date	

Adm Ph.

Email	Psw

Tech Contact Details Name:

Email	Phone

Registrar Name:

Server Details:

1

2

Hosting	Date

User Name.

Psw.

IP:

Name Server

1

2

Comments

Password Diary

Notes

Password Diary

Remember to keep your information in a safe place

Sincerely
YESWORKATHOME.COM

www.ingramcontent.com/pod-product-compliance
Lightning Source LLC
Chambersburg PA
CBHW061506180526
45171CB00001B/61